Survival
KOREAN

처음 시작하는 한국어
Survival Korean

지은이 Stephen Revere
펴낸이 안용백
펴낸곳 (주)넥서스

초판 1쇄 발행 2005년 1월 25일
초판 13쇄 발행 2014년 8월 20일

2판 1쇄 발행 2015년 8월 25일
2판 2쇄 발행 2015년 8월 30일

출판신고 1992년 4월 3일 제311-2002-2호
121-840 서울시 마포구 양화로 8길 24
Tel (02)330-5500 Fax (02)330-5555

ISBN 979-11-5752-346-7 18740

저자와 출판사의 허락 없이 내용의 일부를
인용하거나 발췌하는 것을 금합니다.
저자와의 협의에 따라서 인지는 붙이지 않습니다.

가격은 뒤표지에 있습니다.
잘못 만들어진 책은 구입처에서 바꾸어 드립니다.

www.nexusbook.com

Stephen Revere

넥서스

To my parents, John and Cathey Revere. Though an ocean apart,
your support has always been with me, and it has been the stable foundation
that has allowed me to pioneer into foreign territory.

Preface

I wrote this book out of a frustration that I felt myself as a learner of Korean. When I started learning Korean in 1995, I was taught things that seemed to elicit nothing but laughter from my Korean friends. Words that would only be used in formal situations, things that only grandparents would say, and uncommon expressions seemed to make me humorous when I simply wanted to communicate. Cultural lessons seemed always to focus on Korean traditional dress which I never saw anyone wear, traditional music I never heard, and superstitions that no one any longer believes. As I got better at the language, I realized that there is a wide gap between what most Korean teachers want to teach and what most Korean learners want to learn. This book is an attempt to bridge that gap.

This book is the result of not only my effort, but all the efforts of people who have invested so much of their time to teaching Korean to people like me. I want to thank first and foremost my professors of Korean who have dedicated their lives to teaching this language to learners. Seung-hae Kang began teaching me Korean when I could barely complete a sentence in 1997 and saw me through my graduation from Yonsei University Graduate School of Education in 2004. I can't thank you enough for all you have done for me in Korea. I also want to thank Bong-ja Baek and Ha-soo Kim for their guidance in graduate school and their mentoring since. Each of these professors has decades of experience teaching Korean to learners and I feel honored to have been a recipient of their tutelage. I also want to thank all the numerous teachers at institutes and universities that I studied at over the years.

I am forever indebted to my proofreader and 학교 선배, Jae-hee Jin, for all her assistance with this book. Her meticulous inspection and creative suggestions have made this a much better book than I could have ever written without her help. My appreciation also goes to the folks at Comma 'n Dot; Kwang-hae Hwang and Ji-hwan Kim. They had faith in me before anyone else and have stuck with me through my degree and beyond. I want to thank Robin Berting, Charles Meek and Rich Skimin for their detailed feedback on my manuscript. And to all my classmates without whose support I could never have managed to graduate from a Master's program conducted in my second language, especially Hye-sook Yoon, Bu-mo Kwak, Seung-ju Baek, and Jong-hyun Seo. I thank you for being such amazing friends and your dedication to Korean education.

Nexus Publishing has been nationally renowned for top-quality language textbooks for years. This, however, is their first attempt at a language textbook for their national language. It is fantastic that they are investing in Korean education, and I'm honored that they chose me to be the author of their first attempt. I want to thank Young-hee Jin, Hyun-mi Chey and Mi-hyun Jang for their hard work.

Stephen Revere

"Without language, one cannot talk to people and understand them;
one cannot share their hopes and aspirations, grasp their history, appreciate their
poetry or savour their songs. I again realized that we were not different people with
separate languages; we were one people, with different tongues."

- Nelson Mandela, *The Long Walk to Freedom*

· · ·

"언어 없이 사람과 이야기하고 서로 이해할 수 없고, 남들의 희망과 열망을 동감할 수 없으며
그들의 역사를 이해하고 그들의 시와 노래의 가치를 알아 볼 수 없다.
나는 우리가 상이한 언어를 사용하는 다른 인간이 아니라
다른 언어를 사용할 뿐 같은 인간이란 것을 또 깨달았다."

- 넬슨 만델라, 〈The Long Walk to Freedom〉

Foreword

I first met Stephen Revere in 1997 when he was my student studying at the intermediate level of an intensive Korean program. While not the best student in the class, his enthusiasm for Korean was unmatched. He always kept us entertained with his distinctive humor and occasional outbursts. He also managed to invest a great deal of time socially with Korean people, which has helped him overcome the challenges that Westerners face in learning Korean. His humor, understanding and ability to adapt have helped him blend in a society very different from his own.

All of these talents emerge in this book as well. The context provided for each of the dialogs makes them easier for students to retain in memory. The explanations are written with an obvious appreciation for the challenges that students face in learning this language. The cultural tips in Understanding the Korean World give students the background information necessary to understand and become accustomed to the Korean lifestyle. And through it all his humor is always present, making sure once again students are entertained while learning at the same time.

This book is a great addition to the limited amount of Korean study materials and will be helpful to any beginner trying to approach this challenging language.

Dr. Seung-hae Kang
Graduate School of Education
Yonsei University

📖 Why This Book?

After a decade of teaching English, a decade of Korean study, and graduating as the first native English speaker with a degree in Teaching Korean as a Second Language from the most renowned university in Korea for Korean language education, I've learned a couple of basic things which seem like common sense, but sadly are all too often overlooked by both textbooks and teachers alike. The first is that when students take pleasure in and immediately benefit from what they are learning they work harder, learn more, and are more resolute in their studies. The other is that the more directly relevant the learning is to students, the better they remember it. These two related concepts underlie all of the lessons in this book. Here are some of the ways you'll see them applied:

Most importantly this book will teach you the most practical and commonly used language in Korea. It will teach you words and phrases that you can use immediately. Most other Korean books start with impractical, uncommon expressions and phrases based on the idea that you should learn rules first and language second. This book teaches you practical, everyday Korean and then gives you clear, comprehensible explanations. When a child learns a language they hear it and use it first, and then they learn the rules. That's what this book does too.

While giving you the most common and practical language available, this book will also teach you the structure of the Korean language. Unlike guidebooks or phrasebooks, this book gives you an understanding of the "hows" and "whys" of Korean. Coming from the unique perspective of a native English speaker this book fills in the gaps between the Korean thought and the foreign viewpoint.

Another key to this book is the cultural tips it provides. While other books have culture tips that discuss a Korea long since past, this book talks about 21st century Korea. It shows the linguistic and cultural differences that make learning a language so enjoyable and gives you helpful tips on how to behave with Korean people. A language is as alive as the people who speak it, live it and breathe it. It is precisely by appreciating, enjoying and sometimes even laughing at the differences in cultures that we make learning a language one of the most gratifying experiences there is.

One other feature that distinguishes this book from others is that it provides a real story: a real context for all the material. Instead of disjointed grammar lessons and vocabulary, this book is the story of John, a learner of the Korean language. As you read and hear about John and his arrival in Korea, through the cold Korean winter and even on a trip to lovely Chejudo, you will be able to relate to his situation and imagine yourself living "in Korean" as well.

All of these strategies are combined in order to provide you with a totally new and innovative book for learning Korean.

How to Use This Book

The basic intention of this book is to teach Korean in a way that relates to the non-Korean's experiences. "The Hermit Kingdom," as Korea has been called, is a different world from what learners are generally used to, and it often has a difficult time explaining itself in terms that the novice can understand. Communication is the goal of any language and communicating involves more than just knowing words and phrases. It is a matter of comprehending differences in customs, cultural practices, etiquette and thinking as well. Knowing these deeper characteristics allows for greater insight, mutual understanding and improved interaction.

Read Korean Script in Four Hours teaches you Han-geul, the Korean writing system. The writing system is perhaps the clearest in the world, but up to now books and teachers have presented excessive quantities to students in a single session, leaving students bewildered instead of astonished at its simplicity. With this book's visually-oriented, gradual approach, in only four hours students will be able to read basic Korean script.

After the writing system is covered, study of the language itself begins. It takes place in story form, thereby providing a memorable context for each dialog. **The first page of each chapter is dedicated to activating the student's prior knowledge and giving some essential words and phrases helpful to understanding the dialog.** The pictures aid comprehension by providing visual images of what is taking place. This background provides soil that allows the roots of learning to take hold.

The second page of each chapter is the main dialog. This dialog consists of the most common language that novices are likely to be exposed to, and provides the roots for further instruction and

growth. There is consistent recycling of previously taught vocabulary and grammar patterns to reinforce learned material. Immediately under the dialog is a direct translation which allows students to quickly find the closest English word for the Korean vocabulary in the dialog. Finally the dialog is translated into natural English to provide the overall meaning, which is often different from what it may appear to be in the direct translation.

Following the dialog, *Key Expressions* are given, often in a simplified form. While the dialog is given mainly for comprehension, these expressions are given to aid in production. They are expressions that will be useful to memorize and be able to produce on demand. Student creativity begins to sprout at this point. Then the words from the dialog are given in their basic form.

In the *Getting It* section, clear explanations are given for what was presented in the dialog. The topics given include Pronunciation Rules, Conjugation Rules, Conjunctions, Sentence Endings, and Korean Keys. Korean Keys outline the idiosyncrasies of Korean and allow the learner to understand the likely differences between Korean and their own language. Knowing and understanding these inductive principles allows you to branch out and vary your production of Korean.

***Understanding the Korean World* gives concrete, entertaining examples of the behavior and thought processes of the Korean people and makes approaching and understanding Korean culture easier.** These lessons help the learner communicate and make a better impression on the Korean people they meet, culminating in more fruitful interaction.

Contents

Preface 6
Foreword 9
Why This Book? 10
How to Use This Book 12

Read Korean Script in Four Hours 16
[Study Tip] Every Korean Is a Teacher, the Country Is a Classroom 40

Chapter 1   몰라요 I don't know 44
Chapter 2   깎아 주세요 Give me a discount 52
Chapter 3   화장실이 어디에 있어요? Where's the bathroom? 62
Chapter 4   만나서 반갑습니다 Nice to meet you 74
Chapter 5   좋은 생각이에요! Good idea! 84
[Study Tip] DVDs With Captions 94
Chapter 6   배가 고파요 I'm hungry 96
Chapter 7   고기를 빼고 주세요 No meat please 106
Chapter 8   너무 매워요 It's too spicy 116
Chapter 9   한국말 잘 못해요 I can't speak Korean well 126
Chapter 10 세워 주세요. 내릴게요 Stop please. I'm going to get out 136
[Study Tip] Koreans Aren't Always Right! 146

Chapter 11　전데요. 누구세요? It's me. Who is this? ⋯⋯⋯⋯⋯⋯⋯⋯⋯⋯⋯⋯⋯⋯⋯ 148

Chapter 12　알았어요. 이따 봐요 I get it. See you a little later ⋯⋯⋯⋯⋯⋯⋯ 158

Chapter 13　죄송합니다, 손님 Sorry, customer ⋯⋯⋯⋯⋯⋯⋯⋯⋯⋯⋯⋯⋯⋯⋯⋯ 168

Chapter 14　봄이 금방 올 거예요 Spring will come soon ⋯⋯⋯⋯⋯⋯⋯⋯⋯⋯⋯ 178

Chapter 15　도움이 안 돼요 It doesn't help ⋯⋯⋯⋯⋯⋯⋯⋯⋯⋯⋯⋯⋯⋯⋯⋯⋯ 188

[Study Tip]　Watch Out for Transference Errors! ⋯⋯⋯⋯⋯⋯⋯⋯⋯⋯⋯⋯⋯⋯⋯⋯ 198

Chapter 16　얼마나 걸려요? How long does it take? ⋯⋯⋯⋯⋯⋯⋯⋯⋯⋯⋯⋯⋯ 200

Chapter 17　만으로 서른 살이에요 I'm thirty ⋯⋯⋯⋯⋯⋯⋯⋯⋯⋯⋯⋯⋯⋯⋯⋯ 210

Chapter 18　형제가 어떻게 되세요? Do you have any brothers or sisters? ⋯ 220

Chapter 19　상관없어요 It doesn't matter ⋯⋯⋯⋯⋯⋯⋯⋯⋯⋯⋯⋯⋯⋯⋯⋯⋯⋯ 230

Chapter 20　놀러 오세요! Come hang out with me! ⋯⋯⋯⋯⋯⋯⋯⋯⋯⋯⋯⋯ 240

[Study Tip]　It's All About the Input ⋯⋯⋯⋯⋯⋯⋯⋯⋯⋯⋯⋯⋯⋯⋯⋯⋯⋯⋯⋯⋯ 250

Answer Key ⋯⋯⋯⋯⋯⋯⋯⋯⋯⋯⋯⋯⋯⋯⋯⋯⋯⋯⋯⋯⋯⋯⋯⋯⋯⋯⋯⋯⋯⋯⋯⋯ 253

Index ⋯⋯⋯⋯⋯⋯⋯⋯⋯⋯⋯⋯⋯⋯⋯⋯⋯⋯⋯⋯⋯⋯⋯⋯⋯⋯⋯⋯⋯⋯⋯⋯⋯⋯⋯ 259

Read Korean Script in Four Hours

The Most Efficient Writing System in the World—한글(Han-geul)

Introduction

Hour 1 ㄱ ㄴ ㄷ ㄹ ㅁ / ㅏ ㅓ ㅣ ㅐ ㅔ

Hour 2 ㅂ ㅅ ㅇ ㅈ / ㅗ ㅜ ㅡ

Hour 3 ㅊ ㅋ ㅌ ㅍ ㅎ / ㅑ ㅕ ㅛ ㅠ ㅒ ㅖ

Hour 4 ㄲ ㄸ ㅃ ㅆ ㅉ / ㅘ ㅙ ㅚ ㅝ ㅞ ㅟ ㅢ

Rip Out Cheat Sheet

Conclusion

Introduction

At first glance, to the Western eye there doesn't seem to be a big difference between Chinese, Korean and Japanese writing. People are often astounded that I can read Korean so easily. I find this reaction amusing; if they only knew. Korean is easier to read and pronounce than English. Pronunciation of words is exactly as written; all you have to do is learn the pronunciation of the letters and some rules for the few. Whereas, when I learn a new English word it often could have a couple of different pronunciations, Korean can only have one. That's why I can confidently say that Korean is the simplest and most scientific writing system in the world.

How did it get to be so simple? Way back in the 15th century there was a visionary leader of Korea: King Sejong. At the time Korea used the same writing system as China: pictographs that you had to memorize for each and every word. People spent decades learning characters so they could pass exams to become public servants. Then King Sejong decided that he wanted his populace to be able to read and write, so he commissioned his scholars to create a simple writing system that all of his people would be able to read. Like all visionaries he met with incredible resistance from both scholars and the nobles of the period: the Yang-ban (양반). They didn't want the people to be able to read and write and even feared open revolt if they were educated. Fortunately the King won out.

Today Chinese characters are hard to come by in Korea, unlike China and Japan which still use them predominantly. Korea also boasts the highest literacy rate in the entire world: 97%. This is a testament to the systematic ease with which Han-geul is learned as well as the value Koreans place on education. Koreans are so proud of their writing system that there is a holiday devoted to it on October 9th.

Han-geul has 24 basic letters. These letters can be combined into double (tensed) consonants or double vowels (diphthongs) as well, adding 16 variants of the original letters for a total of 40 letters and combinations of letters.

Hour 1

For your first lesson, we will cover the most basic format of Korean writing; just like English, it goes from left to right: Consonant, vertical Vowel:

Part of the systematic simplicity of Korean is that each grouping of characters makes a single syllable. No clapping to count the syllables in a word like in third grade English class! Each grouping is a single syllable. It is part of the Yin-Yang philosophy of Confucianism that they made sure that a vowel is paired with a consonant.

Here are your first 5 consonants (in alphabetical order):

ㄱ [g] (pronounced close to a "k" at the beginning of a word—meaning it is slightly aspirated)

ㄴ [n]

ㄷ [d] (pronounced close to a "t" at the beginning of a word)

ㄹ [l] (pronounced between an "r" and an "l" and near a "d", hence Koreans have trouble differentiating between the two when they learn English)

ㅁ [m]

There is a symbolic basis to the shape of these letters as well. The "ㄱ" and "ㄴ" are the shape of your tongue when pronouncing them:

And "ㅁ" is same shape as the Chinese character for "mouth," which is based on the shape of a mouth:

Now, there are vertical and horizontal vowels. As per our first arrangement (CV) I will be teaching you the vertical vowels that go to the right of the consonant:

 "ah" (like when the dentist says, "Open up and say, 'Ahhh.'")

 "ou" as in "ought"

 "ee" as in "sheep" (Sometimes pronounced as the "i" in "ship". This also accounts for the difficulty Koreans face in hearing the difference in these vowels.)

 * "ai" as in "air" (considered a diphthong— ㅏ + ㅣ)

 * "e" as in "edible" (considered a diphthong— ㅓ + ㅣ)

Let's look at some words you will see later in this book that can be made with these sorts of combinations. First try to read them yourself, and then listen to the tape.

가다 to go   마다 every   나라 country

다 all   거기 there   다리 leg(s)

다니다 to attend (work or school)   네 yes

★ Don't worry too much about the pronunciation difference between these two vowels. In modern-day Korean the sound difference is almost non-existent. Even Koreans often can't hear the difference and sometimes confuse the spelling.

머리 head   내리다 to get off, to get out (of a train, bus or car)
내다 to pay   가게 store   기다리다 to wait

For future reference, you may want to notice that "다" goes at the end of all verbs and adjectives (with the exception of a few noun-modifying adjectives) in Korean. Adjectives and verbs end sentences in the same way, as you shall soon see.

Now one challenge that you will have is that you need to follow a specific stroke order when writing these letters. I used to think, "Who cares? I can write them however I want to if they look the same." I was wrong. Once you start getting better at the language and start writing quickly, no one can read it if you write in a different stroke order. And reading a hurried Korean person's chicken scratch is impossible if you don't understand what order they wrote each line in! Trust me.

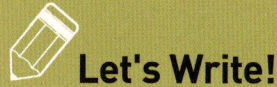 **Let's Write!**

Hour 2

You were probably wondering what I was talking about before with "vertical" and "horizontal" vowels. You see, some of the other vowels come below the initial consonant, making the arrangement:

I know you want to see these so-called "horizontal vowels" but first let me quickly expand your repertoire with four more simple consonants:

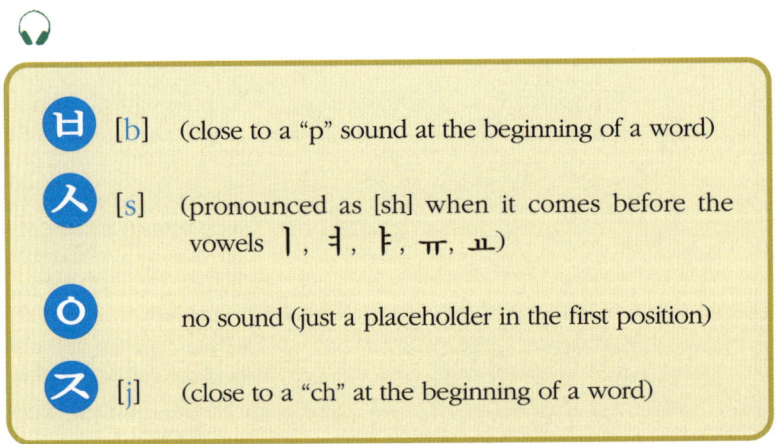

ㅂ [b] (close to a "p" sound at the beginning of a word)

ㅅ [s] (pronounced as [sh] when it comes before the vowels ㅣ, ㅕ, ㅑ, ㅠ, ㅛ)

ㅇ   no sound (just a placeholder in the first position)

ㅈ [j] (close to a "ch" at the beginning of a word)

I know you're wondering how a letter could have no sound, but it makes perfect sense according to the system. You've learned two formats so far, but none of them had a vowel alone, did it? That's because you can't write a vowel all by itself; it must have a placeholder for the initial consonant. Remember that Yin-Yang thing? That's why you must put something in to hold that "C" space. Isn't it nice they chose a big, fat "zero" symbol for us non-Koreans?

And now, just what you've been waiting for: the horizontal vowels. Here you go:

> "oh" as in "Oh, no! I did it again."
>
> "oo" as in "Oops! I did it again."
>
> The Holy Grail of Korean pronunciation for Westerners; Doesn't exist in English, as well as many other languages.

The best help I can give you with the "ㅡ" sound is to say that it is kind of like the sound one makes when one sees something disgusting. The jaw lowers a little we put space between our teeth and let out an, "euh" sort of sound. When it comes between consonants, it's almost like you are trying to pronounce the consonants without a vowel sound in between them. To pick it up listen and repeat the words with this vowel as often as possible. When possible try to watch a Korean's mouth shape and imitate it as well.

Look at that—only four consonants and three vowels! This is the easiest hour of the four and every other letter is really a variation on the 17 letters you have already gotten, so make sure you learn these 17 letters perfectly!

Allow me to give you some words to practice reading with:

누구 who   그래서 So   마시다 to drink
아래 under   N으로 to N   보내다 to send
구 nine   이 two   보다 to see
다시 again   비자 visa   아주 very
어디 where   이다 to be   구두 dress shoes

모자 hat   아이 baby   오이 cucumber
모르다 to not know   비디오 video   사다 to buy
자다 to sleep

✏️ Let's Write!

ㅂ	ㅂ	ㅂ	ㅂ	ㅂ	ㅂ	ㅂ	ㅂ	ㅂ
ㅅ	ㅅ	ㅅ	ㅅ	ㅅ	ㅅ	ㅅ	ㅅ	ㅅ
ㅇ	ㅇ	ㅇ	ㅇ	ㅇ	ㅇ	ㅇ	ㅇ	ㅇ
ㅈ	ㅈ	ㅈ	ㅈ	ㅈ	ㅈ	ㅈ	ㅈ	ㅈ

ㅗ	ㅗ	ㅗ	ㅗ	ㅗ	ㅗ	ㅗ	ㅗ	ㅗ
ㅜ	ㅜ	ㅜ	ㅜ	ㅜ	ㅜ	ㅜ	ㅜ	ㅜ
ㅡ	ㅡ	ㅡ	ㅡ	ㅡ	ㅡ	ㅡ	ㅡ	ㅡ

Hour 3

We've had all the basic letters and the basic setups now. Here come the curves. What if you need a consonant after a vowel? In Japanese, they would start a new syllable and have to add a vowel to it. But in Korean, usually you just add the consonant to the bottom of the prior arrangement. How would this look?

This final consonant is called a padchim (받침), and it is the key to conjugating this language! You must learn to easily recognize syllables with a final consonant and syllables that do not end in a final consonant.

Before we go on to practicing the pronunciation, let me give you the final 5 basic consonants. They're going to look a little familiar:

27

These are the "aspirated" versions of the letters you already learned. Aspiration is the forcing of air out while you make the sound. See how simple this is! It's the same position in the mouth or throat, but you just add a line or write the letter a little differently, and it becomes the aspirated form.

And let's give you six diphthongs (double vowels). This is easy stuff here:

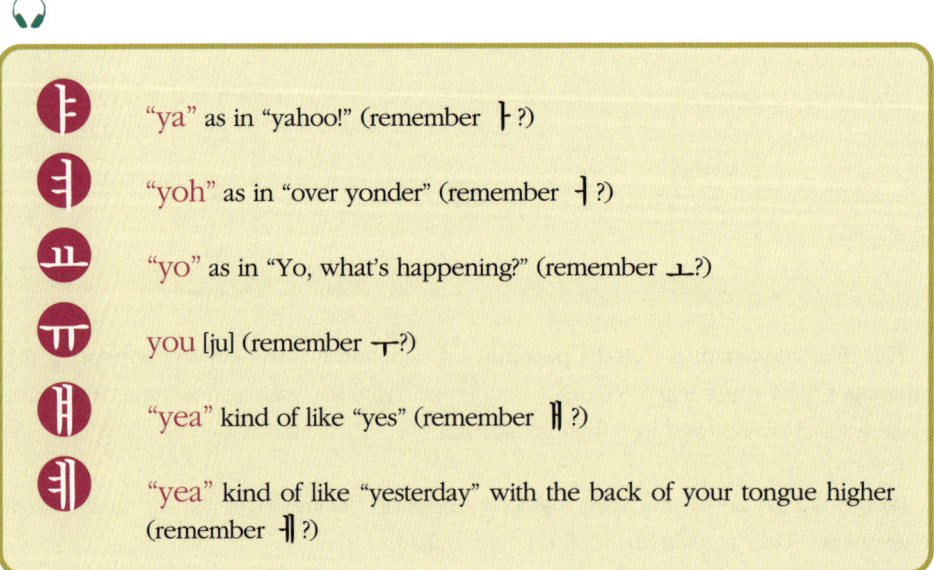

Once again, simply an extra line to make it a slightly different sound. That extra line is like adding a "y" at the beginning of the vowels you already know. Those guys King Sejong got to set this up were pretty smart, weren't they?

Here are some words to practice with:

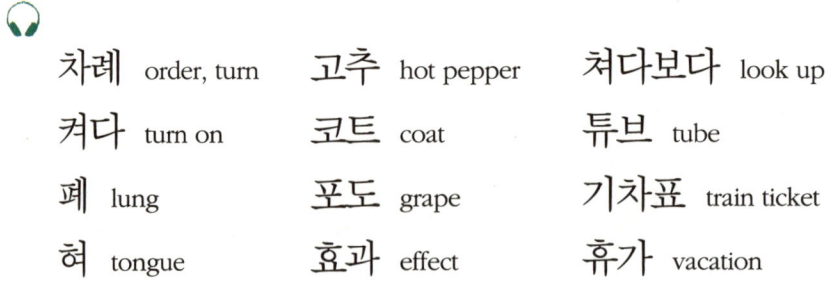

휴게소 rest area   여자 woman   얘기 talk

우유 milk

And now we have to throw you a little twist on what you know already. Let me teach you a new letter:

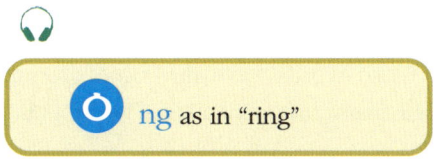

ng as in "ring"

"WHAT! You said that had no sound!" I know, I know. It's not really a new letter. It's an old one with a new rule. When it comes in the initial consonant position there is no sound, it's just holding the space. But when "ㅇ" **comes in the final consonant position (the padchim) then it takes an "ng" sound.** It's a placeholder in the front/top, and an "ng" at the bottom. Some examples:

강 river   영 zero   동 East   방 room   콩 bean

〉〉 Pronunciation Rule

1. Now one other thing complicates this 받침 (padchim) when it is followed by a consonant. **No consonant is aspirated in the 받침 position unless followed by a vowel.** This just means that your mouth holds the same shape, but you don't send air through the space for most sounds. Listen to the following:

먹다 가족 볶다 밉다 부엌 약속 잎

2. Notice that all the "g", "k", "b" and "p" sounds are cut short when they are in the final position and not followed by a vowel. That is not so bad to remember, but this may complicate things a bit. **The sounds of not only ㄷ and ㅌ, but also ㅅ,**

ㅆ, ㅈ, ㅊ, and ㅎ are changed into an non-aspirated "t" sound in the final consonant position if not followed by a vowel. (You'll learn ㅆ in the next lesson.)

Listen to the pronunciation of the following:

있다 맛 낯 및 옷 밑 낫 잊다

Notice that a lot of those words have the same pronunciation despite having different letters in their final consonant. Don't worry, it'll get easier and easier as you see more words.

3 Now I keep using this disclaimer, "if not followed by a vowel." Remember how every vowel must also have that "zero"—the placeholder—in front of it? Well guess what happens when a padchim is followed by that placeholder? Yep, you got it! **When a padchim is followed by a vowel, then the sound moves into the position before the vowel. That's why I often refer to these as padchim enabler vowels.** Look at the following:

옷 – 옷이 [오시]   밑 – 밑에 [미테]
낮 – 낮에 [나제]   한국 – 한국어 [한구거]
맛 – 맛이 [마시]

Starting to get the idea? Trust me, this too will come easily with a little time and study.

Now here are some words for you to listen to and practice reading:

The following is the Sino-Korean number system (there are two sets of numbers):

일 one   이 two   삼 three   사 four
오 five   육 six   칠 seven   팔 eight

구 nine　　　십 ten

These are the pure Korean numbers:

🎧

하나 one　　둘 two　　셋 three　　넷 four
다섯 five　　여섯 six　　일곱 seven　　여덟* eight
아홉 nine　　열 ten

🎧

안녕 hello　　　　　선생님 teacher
여행 travel　　　　한국 Korea
아침 morning, breakfast　　점심 lunch
저녁 evening, dinner

★ This is a double 받침. They're very rare and the consonant pronunciation may vary. You will learn them one at a time. In this case the ㅂ is not pronounced. [여덜]

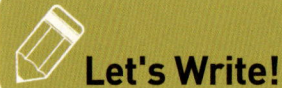 **Let's Write!**

Hour 4

At this point you can read the vast majority of all Korean. I'm sure you've noticed walking around the neighborhood or looking at Korean books that you can sound out almost everything. Well, there are just a few things left that could still throw you, and we're going to go over them today.

First, as usual we have some consonants to add, but they're just variations on the consonants you already know. They're double consonants, and visually they're like seeing double too:

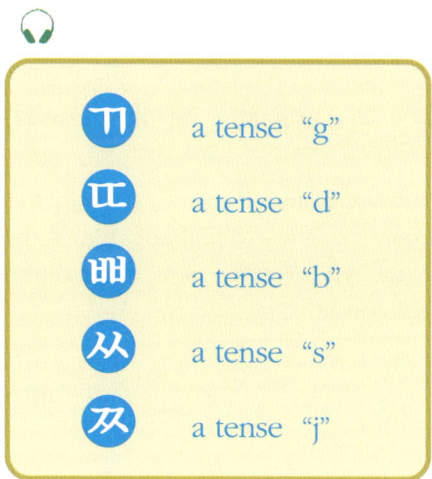

Something else we don't have in English, huh? At first it will be difficult to even hear the differences, but soon it will come to you. I also call it a "hard" consonant. It's kind of like saying the word when you're angry.

Notice that there are plain, tensed and aspirated versions of the same consonant:

Plain	Tensed	Aspirated
ㄱ	ㄲ	ㅋ
ㄷ	ㄸ	ㅌ
ㅂ	ㅃ	ㅍ
ㅅ	ㅆ	
ㅈ	ㅉ	ㅊ

14 of the 19 consonants fit in this pattern, making them very easy to read. The missing five are "l", "m", "n", "ng", and "h" (ㄹ, ㅁ, ㄴ, ㅇ, and ㅎ). Is this efficient, or what?

Have a listen to how these "tensed" consonants sound:

빠지다   깎다   또   뽀뽀   싸다   비싸다   쌀   짜다

And now we have your last group of letters, but sadly they may be the toughest. They are once again double vowels (diphthongs), and they are combinations of vowels you know already. These seven remaining diphthongs have a pattern; horizontal vowel + vertical vowel:

ㅗ + ㅏ = ㅘ   ㅗ + ㅐ = ㅙ   ㅗ + ㅣ = ㅚ

ㅜ + ㅓ = ㅝ   ㅜ + ㅔ = ㅞ   ㅜ + ㅣ = ㅟ

ㅡ + ㅣ = ㅢ

Okay, so you know the math on these letters, but how would they sound?

> 과 "wa" as in "want"
>
> 괘 way [wei]
>
> 괴 way [wei]
>
> 궈 "wo" as in "one"
>
> 궤 way [wei]
>
> 귀 we [wi]
>
> 긔 euh-ee (This English spelling differs from actual Korean pronunciation.)

Listen to the following words:

회사 company
빨리 quickly
외국인 foreigner
원 won (the Korean currency)
뜨겁다 to be hot (to the touch)
봐요. Look.
꿰다 to pass through

의사 doctor
나쁘다 to be bad
위험 danger
깨끗하다 to be clean
왜? Why?
괜찮아요.* It's okay.

★ When a word ends with the ㄶ double 받침, then ㅎ becomes silent and ㄴ moves in front of the 받침 enabler vowel. 괜찮아요. [괜차나요], 많아요. [마나요]

✏️ Let's Write!

ㄲ	ㄲ	ㄲ	ㄲ	ㄲ	ㄲ	ㄲ	ㄲ	ㄲ
ㄸ	ㄸ	ㄸ	ㄸ	ㄸ	ㄸ	ㄸ	ㄸ	ㄸ
ㅃ	ㅃ	ㅃ	ㅃ	ㅃ	ㅃ	ㅃ	ㅃ	ㅃ
ㅆ	ㅆ	ㅆ	ㅆ	ㅆ	ㅆ	ㅆ	ㅆ	ㅆ
ㅉ	ㅉ	ㅉ	ㅉ	ㅉ	ㅉ	ㅉ	ㅉ	ㅉ

과	과	과	과	과	과	과	과	과
괘	괘	괘	괘	괘	괘	괘	괘	괘
괴	괴	괴	괴	괴	괴	괴	괴	괴
궈	궈	궈	궈	궈	궈	궈	궈	궈
궤	궤	궤	궤	궤	궤	궤	궤	궤
귀	귀	귀	귀	귀	귀	귀	귀	귀
그	그	그	그	그	그	그	그	그

Rip Out Cheat Sheet

Consonants (in alphabetical order)

ㄱ	g	(pronounced close to a "k" at the beginning of a word)
ㄴ	n	
ㄷ	d	(pronounced close to a "t" at the beginning of a word)
ㄹ	l	(pronounced between an "r" and an "l" and near a "d")
ㅁ	m	
ㅂ	b	(close to a "p" sound at the beginning of a word)
ㅅ	s	(pronounced as [sh] before the vowels ㅣ, ㅕ, ㅑ, ㅠ, ㅛ)
ㅇ		no sound in first position; "ng" in padchim
ㅈ	j	(close to a "ch" at the beginning of a word)
ㅊ	ch	
ㅋ	k	
ㅌ	t	
ㅍ	p	
ㅎ	h	
ㄲ	a tense "g"	
ㄸ	a tense "d"	
ㅃ	a tense "b"	
ㅆ	a tense "s"	
ㅉ	a tense "j"	

- **Vowels (in the order taught, NOT alphabetical order)**

ㅏ   "ah" (like when the dentist says, "Open up and say, 'Ahhh.'")

ㅓ   "ou" as in "ought"

ㅣ   "ee" as in sheep (Sometimes pronounced as the "i" in ship.)

ㅐ   "ai" as in "air" (considered a diphthong— ㅏ + ㅣ)

ㅔ   "e" as in "edible" (considered a diphthong— ㅓ + ㅣ)

ㅗ   oh (as in "Oh, no! I did it again.")

ㅜ   oo (as in "Oops! I did it again.")

ㅡ   "eugh"

ㅑ   ya (as in "yahoo!")

ㅕ   yoh (as in "over yonder")

ㅛ   yo (as in "Yo, what's happening?")

ㅠ   you [ju]

ㅒ   yea (kind of like "yes")

ㅖ   yea (kind of like "yesterday" with the back of your tongue higher)

ㅘ   wa (as in "want")

ㅙ   way [wei]

ㅚ   way [wei]

ㅝ   wo (as in "one")

ㅞ   way [wei]

ㅟ   we [wi]

ㅢ   euh-ee (This English spelling differs from actual Korean pronunciation.)

Conclusion

Now you have learned all of the written characters in the Korean writing system. It was that easy. Sadly, pronouncing every word perfectly isn't quite that easy. There are double 받침 (padchim), rules for pronunciation of 받침 before certain consonants, contractions, assimilations, forced tensing, et cetera, et cetera. Going into all of the rules here would simply confuse and bewilder you unnecessarily, especially since these rules actually apply to relatively rare circumstances. The good news is that as you continue to learn and be exposed to Korean, you too will encounter these pronunciation rules and you will slowly begin to acquire knowledge of how this language and its writing system are put together. It all comes with time, exposure and perseverance. Keep up the good work.

Study Tip

Every Korean Is a Teacher, the Country Is a Classroom

Most people in the world don't deal with foreigners trying to learn their language on a regular basis. "The Hermit Kingdom," as Korea has been called, is one of those countries with a language that few took interest in learning until Korea's economic boom. Having relatively recently opened up to foreign cultures and people, Koreans are often impressed and flattered by interest in their language and country. This generally makes it easy to get help. Study on the subway or in a crowded coffee shop and sometimes people will offer help without even being asked. If they don't, however, feel free to ask yourself. Most of the time, they will gladly help you with an answer. Another option is a language exchange; you teach them your language and they teach you theirs. That's how I started.

Here are some phrases that will help you when seeking help from a native Korean speaker:

이것이 한국말로 뭐예요? What is this in Korean? *
~이/가 무슨 뜻이에요? What does ~ mean?
이거 뭐라고 해요? What is this called?
방금 뭐라고 하셨어요? What did you just say?

★ This is an irregular version of the proposition N(으)로. It is difficult to pronounce "한국말으로" therefore it is pronounced "한국말로" instead. I think you'll find it much easier to pronounce too.

This book should work especially well in language exchanges; you can explain the English and they can explain the Korean. And in the course of learning I think there will be a lot of cultural discussions that will come up naturally as well!

Meet John!

John has known for a month that he was headed to Korea. Not long ago he graduated from college and started a job hunt. He knew he wanted to try a new country, and he was aiming for something in Asia though he didn't have specific plans for Korea. After spending his last semester of college job-hunting, he managed to land a spot at a company in Korea, making him ecstatic.

The company gave him a month to get ready. That allowed him to study up a little on the language and customs of Korea. He was able to learn all the material provided in this book, and it has made all the difference. He knew better what to expect, he was able to communicate, and he understood a lot of reasons why Koreans do the things they do, as you shall see.

You will be with John as he gets off the plane in Korea, learns his way around and begins to make new friends. As you listen and read, picture yourself in his position, think of what you would say and how you would say it. Because John is of course simply a metaphor: a metaphor for you.

CHAPTER 01 | I don't know
몰라요

John's plane just arrived in Korea and as he exits the plane he says hello and goodbye to a flight attendant who he had talked to during the plane ride. She promptly compliments his Korean, and then asks if he is tired.

Saying "Hi" in Korean is easy. "안녕" actually means "peace," so it's like asking, "Have you been at peace?" to everyone you meet. You must use longer, more polite expressions when talking to older people or people you don't know very well. It's part of a very different and rather strict conception of politeness and showing respect that is based on age and familiarity.

In your first dialog, you will also hear that nearly every sentence ends with the syllable, "요." This is the most common form of saying things respectfully. When in doubt, tack on a "요" at the end of everything you say, just to be safe.

Dialog

존	안녕하세요?
승무원	네, 안녕하세요? 한국말을 잘 하시네요.
존	아니요, 한국말을 잘 몰라요.
승무원	아니요, 잘 하세요. 그런데 좀 피곤하세요?
존	아니요, 괜찮아요. 안녕히 계세요.
승무원	네, 감사합니다. 안녕히 가세요.

John Peaceful are you?
Flight attendant Yes. Peaceful are you? Korean well do wow.
John No, Korean well don't know.
Flight attendant No, well do. But a little tired are you?
John No, okay. Stay in peace.
Flight attendant Yes, thank you. Go in peace.

John	Hello.
Flight attendant	Hi. You speak Korean well.
John	No, I don't know much Korean.
Flight attendant	Sure you do. But are you a little tired?
John	No, I'm okay. Bye.
Flight attendant	Thanks. Bye.

Key Expressions

The vocabulary could be confusing in this chapter. For the first chapter, worry more about memorizing the expressions and how they are used than trying to understand how the parts are put together.

안녕하세요. Hello.

안녕히 가세요. Goodbye. (to someone going)

안녕히 계세요. Goodbye. (to someone staying)

몰라요. I don't know.

한국말을 잘 몰라요. I don't know Korean well.

괜찮아요. It's okay.

감사합니다. Thank you. (Many people seem to want to add "very much" to their "thank you." It may be more polite in English, but it usually just makes you sound like a foreigner in Korean. Try to avoid it.)

안녕 peace   네 yes   아니요 no
한국말 Korean speech   잘 well   모르다 to not know
가다 to go   계시다 to stay (honorific)
피곤하다 to be tired

Bonus Vocabulary

국(國) means country, 사람 means person, and 어(語) means language. Those should help you remember the following:

한국 Korea	한국사람 Korean person	한국어 Korean
영국 England	영국사람 British person	영어 English
중국 China	중국사람 Chinese person	중국어 Chinese
미국 America	미국사람 American person	

Other countries don't have "국" in their names:

일본 Japan	일본사람 Japanese person	일본어 Japanese
캐나다 Canada	캐나다사람 Canadian person	
호주 Australia	호주사람 Australian person	
독일 Germany	독일사람 German person	독일어 German
베트남 Vietnam	베트남사람 Vietnamese person	베트남어 Vietnamese
러시아 Russia	러시아사람 Russian person	러시아어 Russian
프랑스 France	프랑스사람 French person	프랑스어 French
스페인 Spain	스페인사람 Spanish person	스페인어 Spanish

Coming and going

가다 to go   오다 to come

Getting It

⟩⟩ Pronunciation Rule

1 When a 받침 is followed by a 받침 enabler vowel (as signified by the placeholder "ㅇ") the 받침 is pronounced as if it moved into that space.

한국말을 — 말을 [마를]

2 Try saying "습니다" three times really fast. What happens? It becomes difficult to pronounce the ㅂ, doesn't it? It is so difficult that the pronunciation of 'ㅂ' in this formal ending has changed completely. In the formal ending—습니다 the 'ㅂ' is pronounced as a 'ㅁ'.

습니다 [슴니다]

⟩⟩ Korean Key

1 In English, it's not a sentence without a subject, right? You learned it in 3rd grade English class, and most of the time it's true. But notice that Koreans don't use subjects nearly as much as we do. **In Korean often the subject is omitted.**

2 One of the biggest mistakes new learners of Korean make is to constantly say "you" at the beginning of the sentence. In fact, there are a couple of ways to say "you", but both are only used with good friends or when you want to start an argument with someone you don't know well. Don't make the most common mistake for Western learners of Korean! **The pronoun "you" is not used for a subject except with good friends or when talking to young children! When referring to your listener, typically you just omit the subject or use their name (title).** Here are some examples:

괜찮아요. That's okay., I'm okay.

괜찮아요? Are you okay? (Simply raise intonation to make a question.)

Understanding the Korean World

Confucian conceptions of age largely remain to this day in Korea. The elderly rule in any personal situation and almost all professional situations. Rank is very much determined by age. In Korea it is almost unheard of for a boss to be younger than his (her) employees or subordinates. In university the older students who enter first are very much in charge of younger students and may send them on errands for the group like fetching snacks or coffee. And younger people can never, ever be rude or question a senior, even if they have been the recipient of rude remarks or behavior themselves. The flip side of this seemingly unequal relationship is that older people are very much responsible for teaching, training, and taking care of their younger successors. And the best part is, they are usually responsible for the bill. So be careful when inviting out a big group of your younger co-workers or classmates, because you are very likely to be stuck with a large tab!

📑 Exercises

가 Respond the each following Korean sentence.

1. 안녕하세요?

   ☐☐☐☐☐ ?

2. 안녕히 가세요. (You're leaving and they are staying.)

   ☐☐☐■☐☐☐

3. 안녕히 계세요. (You're staying and they are leaving.)

   ☐☐☐■☐☐☐

4. 한국말 잘 하시네요.

   ☐☐☐☐■☐■☐☐☐

5. 안녕히 가세요. (You're both leaving.)

   ☐☐■☐☐☐

🟠 **나** Write the following in Korean.

1. I don't know.

   _____

2. It's okay.

   _____

3. Thank you.

   _____

4. I don't know Korean well.

   _____

5. Hello.

   _____

🟠 **다** Practice the following situation with a friend.

You just saw the most handsome (beautiful) Korean man (woman) you've ever seen in your life. Try saying hello.

CHAPTER 02 | Give me a discount
깎아 주세요

John's friend set him up with a connection in Korea and he is going to meet the young man soon. Since this young man is going to be helping John out he decides to stop by the market to pick a little something up. John ends up going downtown to the world-famous 남대문 market to get his present. After inquiring about the price, John wisely asks for a little discount. All prices quoted are simply a starting place for negotiation at 남대문!

Before you listen, let me remind you of the first five numbers in Korean—일, 이, 삼, 사, 오.

Dialog

존	저기요, 아줌마. 잠시만요. 이거 얼마예요?
아줌마	3만 원이에요.
존	너무 비싸요. 좀 깎아 주세요.
아줌마	그럼 2만 5천 원 주세요.
존	네, 좋아요. 주세요.

John Over there, Madame. A moment only please. This thing how much?
Woman Three ten thousand won is.
John Too expensive. A little discount give please.
Woman Then two ten thousand five thousand won give please.
John Yes, good. Give please.

John	Excuse me, Madame. Can I get a minute? How much is this?
Woman	It is 30,000 won.
John	That's too expensive. Can I get a discount, please?
Woman	Then just give me 25,000 won.
John	Sounds good. Give it to me please. (I'll take it.)

Key Expressions

저기요!, 여기요! Over here! (For getting the attention of strangers in stores or restaurants)

얼마예요? How much is it?

너무 비싸요. It's/That's too expensive.

깎아 주세요. Please give me a discount.

좋아요. Good.

주세요. Please give it to me. (I'll take it.)

여기 here

아줌마 ma'am (polite way to call an older woman you don't know well)

이 this

얼마 how much

원 won (the Korean currency)

너무 too

좀 a little, please

주다 to give

거 thing (abbreviated form of 것)

만 ten thousand

이다 to be (+ noun only)

비싸다 to be expensive

깎다 to cut, to discount

좋다 to be good

➕ Bonus Vocabulary

이것, 그것, 저것 This and that

이 N this N (for objects nearby; especially near the speaker)
그 N that N (for objects nearby; especially near the listener)
저 N that N (for objects far from both speaker and listener)

이것 (이거) this thing   그것 (그거) that thing   저것 (저거) that thing
이 사람 this person   그 사람 that person   저 사람 that person
이곳 this place   그곳 that place   저곳 that place

가격 Price

싸다 to be cheap   비싸다 to be expensive (너무 비싸요!)
바가지 a rip-off   바가지 쓰다 be ripped off (바가지 썼어요!)
값 price   (값을) 깎다 to discount (깎아 주세요!)

색 Colors

노란색 yellow   빨간색 red   갈색 brown
녹색 green   파란색 blue   흰색 white
검은색 black

유용한 동사들 Useful verbs

공부하다 to study   배우다 to learn
받다 to receive, to take, to get

Getting It

>> **Korean Key**

1 You may have noticed that "이다" is translated as "to be", but notice it is specified as only working with nouns. **You do NOT use the verb "to be" with adjectives like you do in English.** You don't say, "That is cheap." You say, "그거 싸." See? No "이다".

2 There are two keys to using numbers in Korean. **Whereas we say "one hundred" or "one thousand" in English, in Korean they almost always omit the "one"**; it's just understood. Of course they don't omit it when they use any numbers other than one—omission is the same as using one, so if you omit it, it is assumed to be one!

Let me show you ~

You make 11 by saying 10 and then 1. 십일

But you make 21 by saying 2, 10 and 1. 이십일

So how would you say 32? That's right. 삼십이

Let's try it with hundreds:

How would you say 111? 백십일

But you have to add 2 syllables to say 555. 오백오십오

Now we'll throw in thousands. How about 1,111? 천백십일

How about 4,100? 사천백

3 In English we count by thousands. That's why the comma goes after every three zeros, right?—One thousand, ten thousand, one hundred thousand. Well here comes the big difference: **in Korean they count by ten thousands!** One ten thousand, 10 ten thousands, 100 ten thousands, and 1,000 ten thousands! A ten thousand is called "만".

So how do you say 11,111? 만 천백십일

How about 60,000? 육만

And how about 300,000? 삼십만

One more—1,000,000

백만—Remember this—a million is 백만. It will be very useful later when discussing numbers, prices and salaries. And it's kind of hard to remember.

Why would I need such high numbers so early in my learning, you ask? Because that green bill that you use constantly in Korea is 10,000 won— 만 원.

〉〉 Conjugation Rule

Conjugating words is much easier than it seems. There is one key to almost all conjugation in Korean—the 받침 (final consonant to a syllable).
When conjugating if a word ends with a 받침, then it is followed by a 받침 enabler vowel. Let's practice this rule with your first sentence ending in Korean.

〉〉 Sentence Ending

1 N이에요, N예요   _to be N

There are two ways to say "it is":

N이에요. (받침 enabler)

and

N예요. (No 받침)

Obviously "이" is a single vowel, so words with a 받침 get ~이에요. "ㅖ" is a double vowel (notice the two vertical lines), so the second form is used when there is no 받침. In today's dialog, 마 of 얼마 does not have a 받침, so "How much is it?"—얼마예요?

And 원 ends in a consonant "n" sound, so for that final consonant to be pronounced clearly, it needs to be followed by a vowel: 3만 원이에요.

Now let's try putting this conjugation rule to work with our second sentence ending.

2 V(으)세요 _Please V

This is the polite command (imperative) ending. Let's try conjugating a verb from the dialog ourselves. The verb 주다 ends in a vowel (ㅜ). Is there a 받침? No, there isn't. It ends in a vowel. A 받침 is always a consonant! If it ends in a vowel, you don't add the vowel in parenthesis:

주세요. Please give me (something).

This time you want to tell someone to receive something from you instead. The verb is 받다. See that 받침 there? It ends in a "d" consonant sound: "ㄷ". In order for that to be pronounced, it needs a vowel added after it: the 받침 enabler vowel! Hence ~

받으세요. Please take this.

It soon becomes habit. Don't worry.

Understanding the Korean World

Never show up empty-handed when invited to a Korean house, but also remember that potluck is not usually the way to go either. In many countries you can show up with something you cooked too, or some sort of side dish, but in Korea the whole meal is usually prepared to blend well together and there are strict rules on what can be eaten with what at a meal (Beer goes perfect with fried chicken, but it doesn't go well with pork according to cultural norms. Corn is excellent on pizza, though!). The best way to go is with flowers or fruit. Flowers are always a nice touch, and if you bring fruit it will probably be eaten after the meal. Fruit after a meal is a very common custom. If you know your host is a drinker, some wine would be nice too.

Exercises

가 You are shopping for a shirt. Ask prices using 이, 그, 저.

나 Politely tell someone to do the following.

보기: Do (it). 하세요.

1. Learn English. _____

2. Go. _____

3. Give (it). _____

4. Study Korean. _____

5. Take (it). _____

다 Write the following numbers in Korean.

1. 725 _____

2. 98 _____

3. 6,538 _____

4. 79,435 _____

5. 549,237 _____

라 Practice the following situation with a friend.

You are wandering around 남대문 and you see a $200 watch being sold for 70,000 won. The problem is you only have 57,000 won. Good luck!

CHAPTER 03 | Where's the bathroom?
화장실이 어디에 있어요?

John made his purchase and is ready to head back to the hotel room, but before that he has a couple of things he urgently needs to take care of. The first is he thinks he'd better find a bathroom before he heads out, but there's none to be found. The other is that he is not quite over his jet lag, so he is starting to feel drowsy. He needs a cup of coffee desperately. Although the major coffee chains have come to Korea, in a place like 남대문 시장 a good coffee shop is still a little hard to find. And to compound his problems John thinks he's running a little bit late, but he doesn't have his watch so he has to ask the time. But don't worry. John knows he just has to ask a friendly Korean face for a little help. Since he has to find a few things, you'll hear him use the word for "where"—"어디" and since he needs to know the time, you'll hear him start out a question, "몇 시"—"What time?"

Dialog

존	저기요, 아저씨. 실례지만, 남자 화장실이 어디에 있어요?
아저씨	저기에 있어요.
존	커피숍은 어디에 있어요?
아저씨	이 빌딩에는 커피숍이 없어요. 옆 빌딩에 있어요.
존	그런데 지금 몇 시예요?
아저씨	5시예요.

John Over there, Man. Rude but, man bathroom where at is?
Man That direction at is.
John Coffee shop where at is?
Man This building at coffee shop not exist. Next building at is.
John And how what time is?
Man 5 hour is.

John	Excuse me. Where is the men's bathroom?
Man	It's over there.
John	Where is a coffee shop?
Man	There is no coffee shop in this building. But there's one in the next building.
John	What time is it right now?
Man	It's 5 o'clock.

Key Expressions

실례지만 Excuse me, but... ("실례지만" is used when interrupting or asking something that might be perceived as rude to **someone you don't know**. Do not use it for asking someone to move or other situations you may use "Excuse me" for in English.)

어디에 있어요? Where is it?

여기에 있어요. It's here.

저기에 있어요. It's over there.

없어요. There isn't one here., It's not here. (Also, "to not have it.")

몇 시예요? What time is it?

실례 a rude act
화장실 bathroom
저기 over there
없다 to not be somewhere, to not exist
빌딩 building
몇 how many

N/V지만 but
어디 where
커피 coffee
그런데 by the way
시 time

남자 man
있다 to be, to exist
숍 shop
옆 next (noun modifier)
지금 now

➕ Bonus Vocabulary

성별 Sex, gender

남자 man   여자 woman

가게와 건물 Stores and buildings

식당 restaurant   레스토랑 restaurant

(Usually a "식당" is an inexpensive and commonly Korean restaurant, while a "레스토랑" is usually used for places that are a little more expensive and/or serve foreign food. This is a tendency. However, it is not a strict rule. You may run into exceptions!)

커피숍 coffee shop

(Be careful of the pronunciation! 코피 means bloody nose!)

편의점 convenience store   슈퍼(마켓) supermarket
백화점 department store   시장 market
은행 bank   도서관 library

음료 Beverages

커피 coffee   차 tea   녹차 green tea
홍차 tea   물 water   우유 milk
주스 juice   콜라 coke

술 Alcohol

맥주 beer   와인 wine   소주 so-ju
양주 (Western) hard liquor

Getting It

〉〉 Postposition

N에 _in/at/to N

English has many different prepositions. Korean makes things much easier in that department because there are very few prepositions by comparison. Actually it has no **pre**positions. Instead it has **post**positions. Be careful; they are attached the word they are describing. "N에" **is used for**

1) the location of something or someone,
2) a destination, or
3) a time

and it is attached after the location, destination or time.

〉〉 Korean Key

1 Saying, "Excuse me"

In today's dialog I taught you one way of saying, "Excuse me, but ...". A '실례' is a rude act, and for Koreans talking to someone you don't know at all can be considered rather rude. But not when you're talking to friends, so only use this phrase when interrupting someone you don't know very well. If you want your teacher's attention, just say, "선생님" — teacher.

One thing that is not so rude, however, is bumping into someone. South Korea is a relatively small country for the size of its population. It is the 13th most densely populated country on the planet, falling behind places like the city-states of Monaco and Singapore, and just behind Taiwan. This, to some degree, accounts for the fact that a little bump here and there doesn't merit asking for an excuse. **When you do need someone to step aside, however, you can say,** "잠시만요." (Just a moment please.)

And finally there are those times when you want to get the attention of clerks, waitresses and other people who should be helping you out. In that case a polite, "Here!" or "There!" will be enough. '여기' is here, '저기' is there, and adding '요' on the end makes it polite.

2 In English we have strict word order because where the word falls in a sentence determines its meaning in the sentence. For instance,
"You moved it"
is very different from
"It moved you."
I switched the subject and the object by changing around their position in the sentence. Korean, especially spoken Korean, does not have the same strict rules, although there are more common word orders (The typical word order is subject-object-verb). The reason is that the subject or object of the verb is determined by "markers." Markers are attached to the word to show who did what to whom. In today's lesson you saw the subject markers and contrastive markers:

이 is the 받침 enabler subject marker

가 is the subject marker attached to words that end with a vowel

은 is the 받침 enabler contrastive/topic marker

는 is the contrastive/topic marker attached to words that end with a vowel

You already saw the object marker. Remember when you learned how to say, "I don't know Korean well."? You said "한국말을 잘 몰라요." — making "Korean" the object of your sentence.

을 is the 받침 enabler object marker

를 is the object marker attached to words that end in a vowel

I know. You're thinking, "I'm okay with this subject marker, and I'm okay with this object marker", but what in the world is this "contrastive/topic marker" thing? Its usage is rather difficult, since its usage depends a lot on the situation. There have been Ph.D. dissertations written on when to use the contrastive/topic vs. subject marker. For now, just remember that it is used to show differences and compare between things. In the case above, you ask about one thing first and use the subject marker, and then you ask about a second thing so you switch to the contrastive marker. Don't worry too much about which one to use yet; Koreans will usually understand if you just use the subject marker. I'll expand on usage differences in later chapters.

3 Let me explain these two crucial verbs in order to prevent future confusion:

★

"있다" is used for

1) Giving the <u>location</u> of something (PL에 있다)
2) Talking about the <u>existence</u> of something (N이/가 있다) and
3) Saying that one <u>has</u> something (PS은/는 N이/가 있다)

"없다" is used for

1) Giving the <u>location</u> that something is NOT (PL에 없다)
2) Talking about NON-<u>existence</u> of something (N이/가 없다) and
3) Saying that one does NOT <u>have</u> something (PS은/는 N이/가 없다)

4 One of the biggest differences between English and Korean is that **they have not one, but TWO ways of counting in Korean. The pure Korean numbers are used for low numbers; always under a hundred.** This may seem like it serves no purpose, but you'll soon see that the distinct usages often make it easy to differentiate what you are talking about.

★ PL=place, PS=person

The pure-Korean numbers up to ten are:

Original form	Irregular noun modifier form
하나	한
둘	두
셋	세
넷	네
다섯	none
여섯	none
일곱	none
여덟	none
아홉	none
열	none

5 Time is more difficult to tell in Korean than most languages. That's because it combines both forms of numbers: the pure Korean numbers for the hours (low numbers: 1–12) and Sino-Korean numbers for the minutes (higher numbers: 1–60). To tell time, **use the pure Korean noun modifier form of the number followed by 시 (meaning o'clock) for the hour and use the Sino-Korean number followed by 분 (minute) for the minutes.**

Hence 1:10 is 한 시 십 분. And 5:45 is 다섯 시 사십오 분. I know that may seem tough at this point, but trust me, I'm speaking from experience here; within a few months it will seem like the most natural thing in the world to you.

한 시 (1시)	오 분 (5분)
두 시 (2시)	십 분 (10분)
세 시 (3시)	십오 분 (15분)
네 시 (4시)	이십 분 (20분)
다섯 시 (5시)	이십오 분 (25분)
여섯 시 (6시)	삼십 분 (30분)
일곱 시 (7시)	삼십오 분 (35분)
여덟 시 (8시)	사십 분 (40분)
아홉 시 (9시)	사십오 분 (45분)
열 시 (10시)	오십 분 (50분)
열한 시 (11시)	오십오 분 (55분)
열두 시 (12시)	

★ Notice that there is a space between the numbers and 시 or 분 when written in Korean letters, but no space when Arabic numerals are used.

Understanding the Korean World

I'm sure that the Korean words for building and coffee shop didn't escape your attention. They are words that have come to Korean through English, and there are many of them. Some of them are used in exactly the same manner as they are in English, and some of them curiously have slightly varied meanings and some have different meanings altogether. This has gained these terms the derogatory label, "Konglish," but let's not look at it that way. English also has adopted many terms from French and other languages that have taken meanings different from the original. Just look at them as new Korean words that make the language richer and more expressive. And make sure you use the Korean pronunciation and not the original English pronunciation; otherwise no one will understand what you are saying!

Exercises

가 Use the correct subject marker.

1. 백화점___ 어디에 있어요?

2. 가게___ 어디에 있어요?

3. 은행___ 없어요.

4. 녹차___ 있어요.

5. 남자___ 없어요.

나 Try writing these phrases in Korean.

1. Ask someone where Australia is.

2. Tell someone there is no Korean person here.

3. Ask someone where a restaurant is.

4. Ask someone where the bathroom is.

										?

다 Write these times in 한글.

1. 3:30 _____

2. 8:27 _____

3. 9:31 _____

4. 11:50 _____

5. 10:10 _____

라 Practice this following situation with a friend.

You have to get to work by 8:30 or you will be fired. You also have to go to the bathroom in a bad way. Ask the guy next to you what time it is and where the bathroom is.

CHAPTER

Nice to meet you

04 만나서 반갑습니다

John has arrived at the arranged meeting place and he's waiting for his host for the evening to arrive. He hardly knows anything about this young man. He doesn't even know his 이름 (name). All his friend told him is that he was a 학생 (student) a few years ago in America. It turns out that the young man's name is 유식 (Yoo-shik). Fortunately 유식 has chosen a place to meet where there are not many foreigners, so it isn't too hard for 유식 to pick him out of the crowd. John and 유식 exchange names and then get to know each other a little more. They're both happy to meet each other.

Dialog

존	안녕하세요? 제 이름은 존이에요.
유식	안녕하세요? 제 이름은 유식이에요. 존 씨는 어떤 일을 해요?
존	저는 회사원이에요. 유식 씨는 어디에서 일해요?
유식	저는 학생이에요. 대학교에서 공부해요.
존	만나서 반갑습니다.
유식	저도요.

John Peaceful are you? My name John is.
Yoo-shik Peaceful are you? My name Yoo-shik is. John Mr. what kind work do?
John I businessman am. Yoo-shik Mr. where at work do?
Yoo-shik I student am. University at study do.
John Meet so happy to see.
Yoo-shik Me too.

John	Hello. My name is John.
Yoo-shik	Hello. My name is Yoo-shik. What kind of work do you do, John?
John	I'm a businessman. Where do you work, Yoo-shik?
Yoo-shik	I'm a student. I study at university.
John	Nice to meet you.
Yoo-shik	Nice to meet you too.

Key Expressions

제 이름은 ~이에요/예요. My name is ~.

어떤 일을 해요? What kind of work do you do?

만나서 반갑습니다. Nice to meet you. (This will be explained in more detail later. For now, just memorize this phrase.)

저도요. Me too.

제 my (formal form)

이름 name

어떤 what kind of

일 work

해요 do (하다, after conjugation)

저 I, me (formal form)

씨 Mr., Ms. (attached after given names, not family names)

회사원 businessperson

학생 student

대학교 university

공부하다 to study

만나다 to meet

V여/아/어서 V so, and then

반갑다 to be happy to see someone

습니다 formal ending (typically used with elderly or very senior persons)

N도 too

Bonus Vocabulary

학교 Schools

유치원 kindergarten 초등학교 elementary school
중학교 middle school 고등학교 high school
대학교 university 학원 institute, academy

Memorize 초, 중, 고 — 초 means first/beginner, 중 means middle/intermediate, and 고 means high/advanced

초급 beginner/low level
중급 intermediate/middle level
고급 advanced/high level

선생 Teachers

선생님 teacher (님 is an honorific ending attached to the end of titles only. A teacher is such an honorable profession that it is almost always attached to this job title unless the person is talking about him/herself.)

강사 instructor 교수 professor (교수님)

직업 Professions, jobs

회사원 businessperson 은행원 bank teller
의사 doctor 간호사 nurse
가수 singer 배우 actor
경찰 police (officer) 비서 secretary

Getting It

〉〉 Korean Key

How to say, 'I' and 'my'

The original polite word for "I" is 저. It is rarely used without a marker of some sort, however. Most often you will hear it with the contrastive marker, because usually when you are talking about yourself you are also speaking in comparison to others, or giving your personal experience.

저는 외국인이에요.

And often you will see and hear that contracted into the shorter form:

전 외국인이에요.

You'll see that the 는 marker is quite often shortened to just adding a ㄴ 받침.

Often you will use the subject marker as well, but when you do remember that you must add an ㅣ on to the end of it. It's not 저가, it's 제가.

제가 외국인이에요.

Then on other occasions, as in the dialog today, it may require that you use a possessive, like "my" or "mine". In that case you just drop that subject marker and place the noun after it.

제 이름은 스티븐이에요.

〉〉 Postposition

N에서 _at / in / on / from N

We've already established that we're in luck on the prepositions. You learned that "에" is used for three things in the Postposition on page 66. Here you learn that "N에서" is the postposition used

1) when giving the location of an action taking place
2) for the location of a starting point or origin

〉〉 Sentence Ending

V여/아/어요 _V

You have mainly been learning the standard "요" form so far. As shown, when verbs are conjugated into regular present tense form, three different vowels can be attached to the root of the verb: V여요, V아요, V어요. The last two you'll learn in the next chapter. The first one is particularly interesting because it is attached to one verb exclusively. "하다" is the most common verb in the Korean language. Common verbs in many languages are often conjugated irregularly, and while Koreans consider "하다" to be a regular verb, it is the only verb conjugated in this manner. **The original form in standard present tense is 하＋여요＝하여요. However "하여요" is nearly always contracted to "해요".** For example,

Tell me what you do:

제가 한국어를 공부해요. I study Korean.

Good. Now I'm going to tell you about my friend, 지환.

지환 씨가 노래를 잘 해요. Ji-hwan sings well.

And I'm also going to tell you what my friends and I do at school:

우리가 학교에서 이야기해요. We talk at school.

Yes, I study when I have to, but I enjoy chatting more.

>> **Auxiliary Article**

N도 _N too

Auxiliary articles connect to the word that they modify. "N도"* means N too. Some examples:

I enjoy Korea. How about you?

저도요. Me too.

I studied hard before, but not so much now. How about you?

저는 지금도 해요. I still do (it).

I try to go to the health club every day. How about you and your friends?

우리도 가요. We go too.

★ Sometimes you will hear Koreans pronounce this as "두" instead of "도". "도" is the correct spelling as well as the correct pronunciation.

Understanding the Korean World

Being polite is an art in Korea, and as a non-Korean if you're good at it, you'll gain respect and influence. If you're bad at it you'll be offending people with every sentence. There are basically 3 levels of politeness: "반말" is the lowest form and it is only used among good friends or to young children. That is unless you want to get into a fight. Next up is what I call the "standard" form; the one that gets that "요" ending. It's the most common at work or in situations where you don't know someone very well. That's the one you're learning right now because it's common and polite. The "formal" form is much less common and used mostly in very formal situations around high superiors, the elderly or to customers (and because you are sometimes a customer you will have to learn to understand it even if you don't use it just yet). Sometimes the levels can mix, however, as you saw in the second to last sentence of today's dialog ("V 습니다" is a formal ending). Don't worry too much about conjugating the other forms yet. Let's try to be "standard" Korean speakers for now.

Exercises

가 Write in the correct postposition.

1. 집___ 있어요.

2. 학교___ 운동해요.

3. 노래방___ 노래해요.

4. 커피숍___ 이야기를 해요.

5. 친구가 여기___ 없어요.

나 Let's try some phrases in Korean.

1. John studies Korean.

2. 유식 works at 남대문.

3. John meets 유식.

다 I've got some questions for you. Answer them in Korean.

1. 한국말을 어디에서 공부해요?

   _____

2. 친구를 어디에서 만나요?

   _____

3. 어디에서 일을 해요?

   _____

라 Practice this following situation with a friend.

Congratulations! The current president of Korea has decided to meet some students of the Korean language in order to understand what kinds of people are interested in Korea and the Korean language. That's right: you've been given an audience with The President! Introduce yourself and tell him a little bit about yourself as well.

CHAPTER **Good idea!**

05 좋은 생각이에요!

John and 유식 are still at their first meeting and they are getting better acquainted. The conversation turns to their interests and 취미 (hobbies). As with many college-age kids in Korea, 유식 is interested in computer games and spends his weekends playing them with his friends. John, on the other hand, isn't a big fan of computer games. He prefers to spend his weekends reading a 책 (book) and watching 영화 (movies). This is good news to 유식, who also really enjoys movies. He suggests that John join him for a movie someday. John thinks that's a fine idea.

Dialog

존	유식 씨는 취미가 뭐예요?
유식	저는 컴퓨터 게임을 좋아해요. 매주 토요일에 친구들하고 게임을 해요. 존 씨는 주말에 뭐 해요?
존	저는 게임을 별로 안 좋아해요. 보통 책을 읽어요. 가끔 영화도 봐요.
유식	저도 영화를 정말 좋아해요. 일요일에 저하고 영화 같이 봐요.
존	좋은 생각이에요.

John Yoo-shik hobby what is?
Yoo-shik I computer game like. Every week Saturday friends with game do. John weekend what do?
John I game not much not like. Usually book read. Sometimes movie too see.
Yoo-shik I too movie really like. Sunday me with movie together see.
John Good thought.

John	What are your hobbies?
Yoo-shik	I like computer games. I play every Saturday with friends. What do you do on the weekend, John?
John	I don't like computer games much. I usually read. Sometimes I see a movie.
Yoo-shik	I really enjoy movies too. Let's go see a movie together this Sunday.
John	Good idea.

Key Expressions

제가 N을/를 좋아해요. I like N.

저는 N을/를 좋아해요. I like N.

주말에 뭐 해요? What do you do on weekends?

별로 안 좋아해요. I don't like it (them) much.

책을 읽어요. I read books.

영화를 봐요. I watch movies.

좋은 생각이에요. Good idea.

취미 hobby   컴퓨터 computer   게임 game

좋아하다 to like   매 every   주 week

토요일 Saturday   친구 friends

들 plural ending (like adding "s" or "es" in English, although not used nearly as much)

만나다 to meet

별로 안 V to not V much, to not V often (only used in negative form)

안 not (negative form)   보통 usually   책 book

읽다 to read   가끔 sometimes, occasionally   극장 movie theater

영화 movie   보다 to see, to look, to watch   정말 really

일요일 Sunday   같이 together   생각 thought, idea

➕ Bonus Vocabulary

취미 Hobbies

컴퓨터 게임 computer game   운동 exercise   영화 movie
춤 dance   노래 song

읽을 거리 Reading material

책 book   신문 newspaper   잡지 magazine   만화책 comic books

매번 Every time

매일 every day   매주 every week
매월, 매달 every month   매년 every year

(월(月) is the Chinese word for "Moon" and so you always use Sino-Korean numbers with it. 달 is pure Korean for month, so you always use pure Korean numbers when counting months with it.)

자주 해요 Do it often

항상 always   보통 usually   자주 often   가끔 sometimes

Memorize these: 월, 화, 수, 목, 금, 토, 일
They are the shortened forms of the days of the week. People often use them, but more often they add "요일" to the end. The days of the week have interesting Chinese origins that may help you remember their names and with other words later:

월요일(月) moon day – Monday (Remember that "month" character?)
화요일(火) fire day – Tuesday   수요일(水) water day – Wednesday
목요일(木) wood day – Thursday   금요일(金) metal (gold) day – Friday
토요일(土) earth, soil day – Saturday   일요일(日) sun day – Sunday

Getting It

>> **Pronunciation Rule**

When a "ㅌ" 받침 is followed by a 이 it is pronounced as a "ㅊ" (ch). I'd love to give you tons of examples of this, but really it applies to only one word I've taught you, so I have to teach you another. 끝 means "end". (Sometimes you will hear Koreans shout out, "끝!" after they are done working.) Now I can give you a few examples:

같이 가요. [가치 가요] (Let's) Go together.

같이 먹어요. [가치 머거요] Eat with us!

끝이에요? [끄치에요] Are we finished?

끝이에요! [끄치에요] Finished!

>> **Conjugation Rule**

1) The standard "V여/아/어요." sentence ending conjugation can seem challenging at first, but it quickly becomes a habit. You already learned the "V여요." option (하다 only) in the last chapter. Now you're going to learn how to choose between the other two. The key is the vowel in the syllable before the ending.

2) If the vowel in the last syllable of the verb stem is ㅏ or ㅗ then it is followed by ~아요.

3) If the vowel is anything besides ㅏ or ㅗ, then it is followed by ~어요.

I know, it seems confusing now, but let's look at some examples with verbs we already know:

읽다 to read—The base of the verb has "I" as its vowel, which falls under rule 3)—it is not ㅏ or ㅗ. Therefore it gets the ending ~어요:

읽어요. [일거요]

좋다 to be good—Now we have a vowel that does fall into the first category—it is an ㅗ! Apply Conjugation Rule 2).

좋아요.

Now some common contractions:

주다 to give—The base of the verb is 주, and the vowel is ㅜ—not an ㅏ or ㅗ, therefore ~

주어요. This is usually contracted to 줘요.

Now, 보다 to see. The vowel in 보 is an ㅗ, therefore it should be followed by ~아요:

보아요. This is usually contracted to 봐요.

Words that end with the 아 vowel are also often contracted because you can't really pronounce 아 twice in a row:

가다 — 가+아요. → 가요.
만나다 — 만나+아요. → 만나요.
사다 — 사+아요 → 사요. (to buy)

〉〉 **Korean Key**

1 There are two ways to make a negative. You'll learn the harder, less casual one in the next chapter, but in today's dialog you saw the easy one. **Place "안" directly before the verb (directly before 하다 in the case of 하다 verbs) to make a negative.**

Today you saw how to say I don't like it:

안 좋아해요.

"좋아하다" is not actually a "하다" verb, it is a combination verb of 좋다 and 하다. Here's a 하다 verb for you.

공부 안 해요. I'm not studying., I don't study.

How about trying, "I am not going / I don't go.":

안 가요.

And finally, "I am not meeting him (or her or them)."

(저는 그 사람을) 안 만나요.*

2 A (으)ㄴ makes an adjective into a noun modifier.

So a good idea is 좋+은=좋은 생각

How about a bad person? 나쁘+ㄴ = 나쁜 사람

And finally, an expensive magazine? 비싼 잡지

★ You don't need the subject or the object for the verb "to meet" like you do in English, as you can see. Many more Korean verbs are "intransitive verbs," meaning they don't need an object.

Understanding the Korean World

When people ask me what the best thing about Korea is I tell them: it's the most fun country on earth. Koreans know how to have fun. Playing computer games with friends at a PC 방 (PC room) is one big pastime, and now there are even professional computer game players that are nearly the equivalent of sports stars. There's even a TV channel dedicated to showing matches. One relatively new phenomenon is the 보드 게임 카페, where you can go with your friends and they will supply you with board games and friendly explanations along with your coffee and snacks. The movie theaters are now state-of-the-art with great popcorn, and when you're not in the mood for a crowd you can always head to a DVD방 and watch a movie with a friend or two in your own private room. And then there's the room that you'll only find in Korea and Japan: 노래방. Koreans love to sing with friends, and there's one understood rule: NEVER criticize someone's singing. That's one reason it's so much fun to go sing with a bunch of Koreans. If somebody's really bad, just bang that tambourine (always supplied) or clap louder.

Exercises

가 Write in the correct marker.

1. 제___ 영화___ 좋아해요.

2. 친구___ 신문___ 읽어요.

3. 존___ 유식___ 만나요.

4. 스티븐___ 공부___ 열심히 해요?

나 Conjugate the following verbs into the 아/어요 ending.

1. 만나다 _____

2. 읽다 _____

3. 좋다 _____

4. 주다 _____

5. 오다 _____

다   Tell me whether you like the following.

1. Do you like 김치?

   _____

2. How do you feel about 운동?

   _____

3. Do you enjoy Korean songs?

   _____

라   Practice this following situation with a friend.

The police have picked you up and are now grilling you on how you spend your free time. It's obviously a case of mistaken identity, but you had better politely answer their questions just the same.

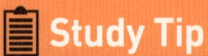
Study Tip
DVDs With Captions

Nothing is better than studying language in context. When you see language in context, you see how it is really used, and one of the best ways to do this is movies. And thanks to the wonderful new technology of DVDs you can now add captioning in English or Korean to the movies that you watch (sometimes Japanese or Chinese as well). I didn't have this kind of a blessing when I was starting out 10 years ago.

Another thing to be thankful for is the explosion of Korean film in the last few years. As recently as the 90s, movies were considered such a risky investment in Korea that they were mostly low-budget, artistic films that lacked mass appeal. But this new century has brought a boom in Korean film and Koreans can be proud of the fact that they are one of only three countries that watch more domestic than imported films. (The other two are India, and of course the US).

The final thing to be thankful for is the Korean custom of the DVD방. I don't know of any other country where you can get your own room to go and watch a movie in. So even if you can't afford a DVD player, you can afford to go check out a movie with captions.

Before you go pick out your DVD, I have some words of advice for you. First, romantic comedies and dramas will have more practical language in them than horror or action movies, but watch what you will enjoy because the more times you watch the movie, the better. Second, it may be a good idea to see the movie with English subtitles first, and then watch it with Korean subtitles. Once you have an idea of what people will be saying it will be easier to recognize the language. And finally, 〈싱글즈〉, and 〈엽기적인 그녀〉 are two of the most enjoyable movies I've ever seen.

CHAPTER 06 I'm hungry
배가 고파요

John just got to Korea, so of course he wants to go do some 구경 (sightseeing). He tells 유식 that he wants to go to 인사동. 인사동 is an area in downtown Seoul that is famous for traditional Korean arts, crafts and tea houses. It is an essential stop on any tour of this great city. 유식 doesn't mind, but he thinks it will be 복잡하다 (crowded) right now so they should head over a little later. It turns out after some questioning that 유식 has other reasons as well. He is 배고파요 (hungry). Fortunately John is too, so their next order of business is getting something to eat.

Dialog

유식	이제 뭐 하고 싶어요?
존	인사동을 구경하고 싶어요.
유식	지금은 인사동이 복잡하니까, 조금 이따가 가요.
존	유식 씨는 뭘 하고 싶어요?
유식	저는 배가 고파요. 뭘 좀 먹고 싶어요. 존 씨는요?
존	저도 배고파요.

Yoo-shik Now what do want to?
John Insadong sightseeing do want to.
Yoo-shik Now Insadong crowded because, a little later go.
John Yoo-shik what do want to?
Yoo-shik I stomach hungry. Something a little eat want to. John?
John I too stomach hungry.

Yoo-shik	What do you want to do now?
John	I want to sightsee around Insadong.
Yoo-shik	Right now, since it's crowded in Insadong, let's go a little later.
John	What do you want to do?
Yoo-shik	I'm hungry. I want to eat a little something. How about you?
John	I'm hungry too.

Key Expressions

뭐 하고 싶어요? What do you want to do?

구경하고 싶어요. I want to go sightseeing.

이따가 가요. Let's go a little later.

N에 가고 싶어요. I want to go to N.

먹고 싶어요. I want to eat.

배가 고파요. I'm hungry.

이제 now (shows contrast with the pasts)

V고 싶다 to want to V　　　구경하다 to sightsee

인사동 a traditional crafts market in Seoul

복잡하다 to be crowded (also means "to be complicated")

V(으)니까 because V　　　조금 a little

이따가 later　　　배 stomach

고프다 to be hungry (always attached to "배(가)")

뭘, 무엇을 what (objective form)　　　좀 please

Bonus Vocabulary

시간에 대한 부사 Adverbs about time

이따가 a little later
금방 soon
조금 전에 a little while ago
나중에 later (not used for the near future)
아까 a minute ago
예전에 a long time ago

Stomach states

배고프다, 배가 고프다 to be hungry (배고파요.)
배부르다, 배가 부르다 to be full (배불러요.)

먹는 것에 대한 동사 Eating-related verbs

굶다 to starve, to skip a meal   과식하다 to overeat

몸 Body

눈 eye(s)   코 nose   입 mouth   귀 ear(s)
다리 leg(s)   팔 arm(s)   머리 head   목 neck, throat
가슴 chest   엉덩이 bum, buttocks

Getting It

>> **Sentence Ending**

So you want to know how to say "want"? I can't help you there. I'll only teach you "want to". Here's the thing. Koreans don't often use want + N, the way we do in English. There is a word for it, but if you use it when you're starting, nine times out of ten people just look at you funny. You don't say, "I want a burger." You say, "I want to eat a burger." "**V고 싶다**" **is the equivalent of** "**to want to V**". Notice that the nice thing about this ending is there is no conjugation required. Just add the ending to the verb stem of your choice. So how do you really tell someone that you want a hamburger?

햄버거를 먹고 싶어요.

And after you've eaten, I'll bet you want to get some exercise:

운동하고 싶어요.

Is it time to relax now?

네, 쉬고 싶어요.

What do you want to do to relax?

책을 읽고 싶어요.

And what do you want to do after you're done reading?

영화를 보고 싶어요.

>> **Irregular verb**

"으" omission

Here's an easy irregular verb for you. Just drop the last letter. **When the last syllable of a verb ends with** "으" **and is conjugated into the polite 아/어요**

form, then the "으" is dropped and the 아/어요 ending is added according to the vowel in the previous syllable. You saw this in the first expression today. I'm hungry:

배가 고프다 → 배가 고프 + 아요 → 배가 고파요.

Now you also learned in the last chapter that a bad person is 나쁜 사람, but what if you just want to say, "He's bad."

나쁘다 → 나쁘 + 아요 → 나빠요.

And what if there's only one syllable? There is no previous syllable to determine whether to add 아 or 어 before the 요, like in the verb for "to write" — 쓰다. Then what do you do?

쓰다 → 쓰 + 어요 → 써요.

See, it's not so bad. If there's no "오", or "아", then end with "어요".

》 Conjunction

V(으)니까 _because V

There are a couple of ways to give reasons for something in action in Korean, and they're used a little differently. You saw one today when 유식 suggested that they go to 인사동 later because it's crowded right now. V(으)니까 is **used for giving the reason for doing something—especially personal reasons, commands, suggestions and proposals.** So let's start out with a personal reason. Why did you buy this book?

한국말 잘 하고 싶으니까 샀어요.

Good reason (and good choice). Now in today's dialog, 유식 makes a suggestion (notice the simple present tense can be used to make suggestions). He doesn't like crowds so he floats the idea that they should go later~

복잡하니까 나중에 가요.

And finally, I'd like to give you a command, but I'll give you a reason for following the command too ~

한국말이 어려우니까 열심히 공부하세요.

You really do have to study hard, but studying is fun too, isn't it?

〉〉 Korean Key

Periodically from now on you will see that the subject, contrastive or objective markers may be missing. That's because it is often more natural to omit them than it is to put them in. Actually some of the phrases in this book would be more natural without the markers. But since you're just starting out it's better to see them and use them as often as possible. They're kind of like training wheels; once you get good enough you can remove them when appropriate.

Understanding the Korean World

When you're going out to eat with Korean people, you don't decide where to eat; you decide what to eat. In many countries you pick the restaurant first, and then you pick your food from a varied menu and you get your own plate. Not in Korea, where everyone usually eats the same thing. Picky eaters are hard to come by. It's all another part of how people become closer in Korean culture. Many restaurants in Korea, like world-famous Korean barbecue, have only a few things on the menu. Some of the best restaurants I've ever been to in Korea have only had ONE thing on the menu. If they only serve one thing, you KNOW they must do it well! And when I say, "You eat together," I mean you eat **together**. Often soups and side dishes will be shared by all, a practice that seems unhygienic to many people of Western backgrounds. But trust me, after 10 years in this country and sharing countless bowls of hot 찌개 (not to mention 소주 glasses) I don't think I get any more colds than I did back home.

Exercises

가 Try it in Korean.

1. I want to meet that person.

☐☐☐☐☐☐☐☐☐☐☐☐

2. I want to go to the convenience store.

☐☐☐☐☐☐☐☐☐☐

3. I want to study Korean.

☐☐☐☐☐☐☐☐☐☐☐

나 Combine the sentences using "V(으)니까".

1. 그 영화가 좋아요. 보세요.

_____

2. 비싸요. 좀 깎아 주세요.

_____

3. 배고파요. 레스토랑에 가요.

_____

4. 지금 바빠요. 이따가 만나요.

_____

다 Conjugate the following irregular "으" verbs into the "아/어요" form.

1. 나쁘다 _____ .

2. 아프다 _____ .

3. 쓰다 _____ .

4. 배가 고프다 _____ .

라 Practice the following situation with a friend.

Your friend is starving but you are not hungry at all. You really want to see some sights in the area before leaving to get some food. Try to convince your friend to stick it out a little longer.

CHAPTER **No meat please**

07 고기를 빼고 주세요

You're going to hear a lot of formal conversation in today's dialog. That's because John and 유식 are customers in a restaurant now, and retail staff usually use formal and honorific forms when speaking to customers in order to make them feel like they are being highly respected. John also speaks very politely because he doesn't know the waitress at all, which requires extra courtesy on his part. What polite phrasing and slightly higher intonation accomplish in English is done with the different levels of speech in Korean.

You'll hear, "~시겠어요?" a lot in today's expressions. It is the polite way to ask what someone wants or ask someone to do something for you. It's like using, "Would you…?" or "Could you…?"

Dialog

존	여기요! 메뉴를 좀 주시겠어요?
종업원	여기 있어요. *(잠시 후)* 주문하시겠어요?
존	네, 비빔밥 하나요. 고기는 빼고 주세요.
종업원	손님은요? 뭘 드릴까요?
유식	된장찌개 하나 주세요.
종업원	네, 잠시만 기다리세요.

John Here! Menu please give will?
Waitress Here is. *(one moment after)* Order would?
John Yes. Mixed rice one give please. Meat remove and give please.
Waitress Customer? What give shall?
Yoo-shik Fermented soybean paste soup one give could?
Waitress Yes, moment only wait please.

John	Excuse me. Could I have a menu, please?
Waitress	Here you are. *(after a moment)* Would you like to order?
John	Yes. One bibimbap please. No meat.
Waitress	How about you? What can I get you?
Yoo-shik	Could I have twenjang chigae please?
Waitress	Okay. One moment please.

Key Expressions

N을/를 주시겠어요? Could I please have N?

여기 있어요. Here you are.

주문하시겠어요? Would you like to order?

N 빼고 주세요. Give it to me without N please., No N please.

뭘 드릴까요? What can I get you?, What would you like?

잠시만 기다리세요. One moment please.

메뉴 menu

좀 please (original meaning is "a little", but now is the equivalent of "please")

V시겠어요? Could you V?, Would you V? (honorific, polite)

종업원 waitress, waiter

후 after

비비다 to mix

고기 meat

V고 V and

V(으)ㄹ까요? Should (I, we) ~?

된장 a fermented bean paste

기다리다 to wait

잠시 a moment

주문하다 to order

밥 rice

빼다 to remove, to take out

드리다 to give (honorific, 1st person)

드시다 to eat (honorific, 2nd person)

찌개 soup, stew

➕ Bonus Vocabulary

한식 Korean dishes

된장찌개 fermented bean paste soup   김치찌개 kimchi soup
불고기 Pulgogi (a sweet marinated beef)
갈비 Kalbi (marinated ribs)
닭갈비 Chicken Kalbi (a spicy chicken-veggie stir fry)
비빔밥 mixed rice (rice, hot pepper paste, veggies and usually a little meat too)

야채 Vegetables

당근 carrot   양파 onion   파 green onion
상추 lettuce   고추 hot pepper   감자 potato

과일 Fruit

사과 apple   배 pear   딸기 strawberry
포도 grape   오렌지 orange
귤 mandarin orange (much more common than regular oranges)

Animal and meat

소 cow — 소고기 beef
돼지 pig — 돼지고기 pork
닭 chicken — 닭고기 chicken
물 water — 물고기 fish — 생선 fish (for eating)

109

Getting It

>> **Sentence Ending**

1 V(으)시겠어요? _Would you like to V?, Could you please V?

The next step in your Korean learning is asking for something politely. "V(으)시겠어요?" **is the polite way to ask if someone would like to do something.**

보시겠어요? Would you like to see? Okay, here are some examples:

"Could I have something?" When you want to request something in a restaurant, use this form:

N을/를 좀 주시겠어요? ("좀" originally means "a little" but it is just as often used to mean "please" in spoken Korean.)

How about if you want to ask someone, "Would you like to go now?" Try that one:

가시겠어요?

And for one more example, "Would you like to come to the party?"

파티에 오시겠어요?

2 V(으)ㄹ까요? _Should, shall (I, We) V?

When you want to offer to do something for someone or with someone, this is the way to do it. You'll hear this often, especially at restaurants where the workers are constantly offering you something like water ~

물을 드릴까요?

Or when they offer to clear something away for you ~

치울까요?

〉〉 Showing Respect

1 V(으)시

What exactly is happening in that V시겠어요? sentence ending? You're being very polite. One major way you are doing that is adding 시 directly after the verb. You will hear other people do this when talking to you, and you should be aware that they are being extremely polite. **In order to be more polite, attach (으)시 to the end of any verb referring to another person's actions.**

2 Alternate Vocabulary

I'm sure that you also noticed that there are some completely new verbs that you may not have seen before to refer to things that you already know. That's because for some of the most common verbs you have to **use completely different verbs when referring to the other person's action (2nd person):**

먹다 — 드시다* 있다 — 계시다* 자다 — 주무시다*

And to make sure that things are nice and complicated, on some occasions you have to **use completely different verbs to refer to your actions toward the person.**

주다 — 드리다 (1st person)

말하다 — 말씀드리다 (to tell someone something)

And **there are other nouns used when referring to the other person too.**

나이 — 연세 (age)

집 — 댁 (house)

밥 — 진지 (food)

이름 — 성함 (name)

★ Notice that these verbs already end in – 시, therefore you do not add it on a second time.

〉〉 Conjunction

Koreans use verbs together quite often. One of the ways you saw today: **V₁고 V₂ shows two actions that take place in the order given**. Often when you are stepping out for lunch and someone else will be waiting for you to come back, they will tell you:

드시고 오세요.

When ordering and you don't want that spicy red pepper paste, then you say,

고추장 빼고 주세요.

Understanding the Korean World

Rice isn't just a food staple to Koreans. Until only recently it wasn't considered a meal unless there was rice on the table. Even today you'll periodically hear older people prostrating the younger generation, "밥 먹어야지, 밥!" (You gotta eat rice, I tell ya! Rice!) Anything else is just a snack, and this includes hamburgers. In America we talk about being hungry an hour after eating Asian food, and in Asia they talk about being hungry an hour after eating American food. Obviously it's more a matter of being satiated by what you're used to than the number of calories.

It is of central importance to the culture in many ways too. It works its way into many phrases, expressions and even proverbs. One of the most common greetings in Korea is to ask if you ate, but people often don't ask you if you had lunch; they ask you if you had rice! "밥 먹었어요?" And even if you had pizza for lunch, the answer is Yes! That's right; the word "rice" is the equivalent of the word "food" in many instances. So the next time you hear, "밥 먹을까요?" even if you dread the thought of another bowl of rice and nothing would make you happier than a huge plate of pasta, if you're hungry make sure to respond with a big "네!"

Exercises

가 Ask if someone "Would like to V?" using the verbs given.

1. 오다 _____?

2. 가다 _____?

3. 드시다 _____?

4. 주다 _____?

나 Connect the sentences with the conjunction V고 V.

1. 숙제를 해요. 오세요.

   _____

2. 고추장을 빼요. 주세요.

   _____

3. 밥을 먹어요. 만나요.

   _____

다 Ask if you should do the following verbs (V(으)ㄹ까요?).

1. 먹다 _____?

2. 쉬다 _____?

3. 가다 _____?

라 Practice the following situation with a friend.

Let's pretend you're a vegetarian in a Korean restaurant. Order some food, but be careful! Meat and/or meat-based broths seem to make their way into almost every Korean dish. Make sure you order without any meat! (For a real challenge try pretending you can't eat anything spicy either!)

CHAPTER 08
It's too spicy
너무 매워요

유식, as a good Korean host, makes sure that John is enjoying his food. John finds something strange, however. 유식 isn't touching the 김치 (kimchi) on the table. Now, being that this is not just a Korean staple, but that eating 김치 is almost synonymous with being Korean, John inquires as to what's up. Apparently this 김치 is a little 매워요 (spicy). It turns out 유식 isn't so good with spicy stuff while John is, which goes against one of the greatest stereotypes in Korea: Koreans love spicy food and foreigners don't (but it's my book and I love breaking stereotypes!). Fortunately 유식 somehow manages to end up full despite avoiding the 김치. He says he's too full.

Dialog

유식	맛있죠?
존	네, 아주 맛이 있어요. 그런데 김치를 왜 안 먹어요?
유식	김치가 맛이 없어요. 너무 매워요. 존 씨도 맵죠?
존	아니오, 그렇게 맵지 않아요. 저는 이 김치가 정말 좋아요. 그렇지만 조금 짜요.
유식	아휴, 너무 배불러요.

Yoo-shik Taste have, huh?
John Yes. Very taste have. But kimchi why not eat?
Yoo-shik Kimchi taste not have. Too spicy. John too spicy, huh?
John No, that spicy not. I this kimchi really like. But a little salty.
Yoo-shik A-hew. Too full.

Yoo-shik	Delicious, isn't it?
John	Yes, very delicious. But why aren't you eating the kimchi?
Yoo-shik	I don't like this kimchi. It's too spicy. It's spicy, isn't it?
John	No, it's not that spicy. I really like it. But it is a little salty.
Yoo-shik	Whoa, I'm stuffed.

Key Expressions

맛(이) 있어요. It's delicious.

너무 매워요. It's too spicy.

그렇게 맵지 않아요. It's not that spicy.

배불러요. I'm full.

배불러요? Are you full?

맛 taste
맵다 to be spicy
조금 a little
너무 A too A*

아주 very
배부르다 to be full
짜다 to be salty

★ A=adjective

Bonus Vocabulary

맛 Taste

맛있다 [마싣따], 맛이 있다 to be delicious
맛없다 [마덥따], 맛이 없다 to taste terrible
맵다 to be spicy   싱겁다 to be bland
짜다 to be salty   시다 to be sour
달다 to be sweet   쓰다 to be bitter

느낌 Feeling

차갑다 to be cold (to the touch)   뜨겁다 to be hot (to the touch)
춥다 to be cold (air temperature)   덥다 to be hot (air temperature)

식사 Meals

아침 breakfast (also means 'morning')   점심 lunch
저녁 dinner (also means 'evening')

난이도 Difficulty

어렵다 to be difficult   쉽다 to be easy
힘들다 to be exhausting/difficult

Getting It

〉〉 Sentence Ending

1 V죠?   _S, huh? / S, eh?

Canadians have a tendency to add, ", eh?" on to the end of their sentences, as if they are just looking to start a friendly conversation, or confirm that the other person agrees. Koreans do the same thing with the "V지요?" ending. But be careful, you men out there! Saying the full "V지요?" ending can sound a little feminine, so I suggest both men and women use the abbreviated form: **The "V죠?" question ending invites agreement and makes conversation.**

So when you think you're hungry and you think your friend is too, try this:

배고프죠? 먹고 싶죠?

Or you have a feeling that your friend wants to meet that handsome man from the other day and you want to tease her a little:

그 남자를 만나고 싶죠?

How about when you're eating spicy 김치 together, and you want to make sure they are going through the same torture that you are:

김치가 맵죠?

Sometimes Koreans will finish a sentence and then just add a new sentence entirely:

찌개가 너무 뜨거워요. 그죠?

I suggest trying to throw "그죠?" on the end of some observations every once in a while. Then you'll really sound like a Korean.

2 V/A지 않다 _to not V, to not be A

We learned one form for making the negative already, didn't we? What was that again? Oh, yes. '안' before the verb. Here's another negative, but this one comes after the verb and is used in more formal and written Korean while '안' is more colloquial. 'V/A지 않다' **means to not V / to not be A**. We saw a negative question today:

맵지 않아요? Isn't that spicy?

And I'm curious. Do you find Korean difficult?

쉽지 않아요.

Yeah, it's not so easy, is it? Now a friend wants to know if you're busy— 바빠요? But you're not busy:

바쁘지 않아요.

You always have time for your friends, right?

》 Irregular Verb

1 Irregular 'ㅂ' verbs

The great thing about irregular verbs in Korean is they have rules, unlike in many other languages where you just have to memorize all the different forms. I guess that kind of makes them regular in some fashion. Anyway, I'm sure you noticed that in today's Bonus Vocabulary there are many words ending in "ㅂ." Remember, not all verbs ending in "ㅂ" are irregular; a few of the verbs ending in "ㅂ" are regular.

When a transforming "ㅂ" verb meets a vowel, then the "ㅂ" changes into an "우" and also replaces any 받침 enabler vowel.★ **When a "ㅂ" irregular meets a consonant, there is no change.**

★ except for the two verbs 돕다 (to help) and 곱다 (to be attractive in a country-girl-next-door sort of way) where it changes to an "오" in the V여/아/어 conjugation, but it still changes to "우" before any 받침 enabler vowel

121

You of course need some examples to understand this rule. Let's try saying it's difficult in the polite form:

어렵다 → 어려 + 우 + 어요 → 어려워요

한국말이 어려워요.

Maybe you disagree. Maybe you think this is easy:

쉽다 → 쉬 + 우 + 어요 → 쉬워요

영어가 쉬워요.

And of course you have to remember this phrase in Korea because quite often the food is so incredibly spicy:

맵다 → 매 + 우 + 어요 → 매워요

김치가 매워요.

But before a consonant it stays the same:

맵죠?

2 Irregular '르' verbs

You've learned one of these already. Remember in the first chapter when you learned how to say, "I don't know Korean well." That was an example of this irregular. When "르" verbs meet the standard, V아/어요 form, the "ㅡ" is dropped, the "ㄹ" is doubled and the appropriate ending is added. Watch:

모르다 → 모르 + 아요 → 몰ㄹ + 아요 → 몰라요

You add "아요" because of the "오" in 모. What would happen if it were not an "아" or "오" in the first syllable? Then of course you would have to add "어요." ~ as in the phrase for "I'm full."

배부르다 → 배부르 + 어요 → 배불ㄹ + 어요
→ 배불러요

Understanding the Korean World

A typical Korean dinner table can seem bewildering to a newcomer. Dishes are spread out all over the place and you may not know when you're eating your food or when you're stealing someone else's food. Let me give you the basics.

Usually there is a main dish (typically a soup or stew; sometimes meat) that is shared by all. There are also many side dishes called 반찬, and these are also shared by all. You get a bowl of rice, a soup bowl which goes to the right of the rice, chopsticks and a spoon all for your own. And remember that the spoon is for the rice! You may have seen Asians on TV scooping rice into their mouths with chopsticks before, but they weren't Koreans! The Japanese and Chinese sometimes eat that way, but Koreans use their spoons for rice and soup. The chopsticks are usually metal chopsticks too, which can be a little more challenging than the wooden or plastic chopsticks you're used to. You'll get the hang of it.

You may also find that Koreans eat unbelievably fast. That's what happens when you grow up in a culture where you eat most of the dishes together. The fastest eater gets the most!

Exercises

가 Make a friendly observation with the following verbs.

1. 어렵다 _____?

2. 맛있다 _____?

3. 맵다 _____?

4. 모르다 _____?

나 Conjugate the following verbs into the 아/어요 sentence ending.

1. 어렵다 _____

2. 쉽다 _____

3. 모르다 _____

4. 빠르다 _____

다 Make the statements negative using V지 않다.

1. 배불러요. _____

2. 뜨거워요. _____

3. 더워요. _____

4. 힘들어요. _____

라 Practice the following situation with a friend.

What kinds of foods do you like? Discuss with a partner the foods that you enjoy.

CHAPTER **09** I can't speak Korean well

한국말 잘 못해요

John had a wonderful time hanging out with 유식. He was a little younger, but they turned out to have the same taste in movies and books, which led to some great conversation. Now John has to head home and he knows it's not far, so he decides to go with a taxi. Three key words will pop up that you have to know if you don't know them already: 직진, 오른 and 왼. 직진 sounds very different, so it's probably easier to remember that it means "straight," but it may be tougher with 오른 (right) and 왼 (left). Just remember there are two syllables to a right turn and one syllable left. Oh, and you'll also hear them say not just 오른 but 오른쪽, and not just 왼 but 왼쪽. You have to add "쪽" when talking about directions or sides.

Dialog

택시 기사	안녕하세요? 어디 가세요?
존	안녕하세요? 직진해 주세요. 코너에서 오른쪽으로 가 주세요.
택시 기사	네. 다음에는요?
존	저기 앞에서 왼쪽으로 가 주세요.
택시 기사	와, 우리말 잘 하시네요!
존	한국말 잘 못해요.
택시 기사	아니요, 정말 잘 하세요.

Taxi driver Peaceful are you? Where go please?
John Peaceful are you? Straight do please. Corner at right direction go please.
Taxi driver Yes. Next what about?
John Front in left direction go please.
Taxi driver Waa, Korean speech well do (I'm surprised.).
John Korean well can't do.
Taxi driver No, really well do.

Taxi driver	Hello. Where to?
John	Hello. Go straight please. At the corner turn right.
Taxi driver	Okay. And then?
John	Up there take a left please.
Taxi driver	Wow, You really speak Korean well!
John	I can't speak Korean well.
Taxi driver	No, you really do speak well.

Key Expressions

직진해 주세요. Please go straight.

오른쪽으로 가 주세요. Please turn right.

왼쪽으로 가 주세요. Please turn left.

한국말 잘 못해요. I can't speak Korean well.

정말 잘 해요. You really do it well.

택시 taxi

V(으)세요? polite question ending

직진하다 to go straight (notice it's 하다! NOT 직진으로!)

V여/아/어 주다 to V for someone

코너 corner

쪽 direction, side

다음 next

앞에 in front

와 Wow

잘 well

기사 driver

오른 right

N(으)로 to (somewhere)

은/는 what about

왼 left

한국말 Korean (speech)

V네요 ending showing surprise

Bonus Vocabulary

교통 Transportation

택시 taxi   버스 bus   지하철 subway
기차 train   비행기 plane
배 ship (That's right ~ '배' means ship, pear, and stomach!)

방향 나타내기 Giving directions

오른(쪽) right (side/direction)   왼(쪽) left (side/direction)
앞(쪽) front (side/direction)   뒤(쪽) back (side/direction)

교통 관련 동사 Transportation verbs

타다 to ride   뛰다 to run
걷다 to walk   조깅하다 to jog
운전하다 to drive   산책하다 to go for a walk, to take a walk

위치를 나타내는 후치사 Postpositions of location (In English they are prepositions but in Korean they come after the object, so they are postpositions.)

앞에 in front of   뒤에 behind   옆에 next to
위에 above   아래에 below, under
안에 inside   밖에 outside   사이에 in between

Getting It

〉〉 Auxiliary

1 **N(으)로 is added to directions or destinations.** It's a lot like adding the preposition "to" on the end of a destination. There's a great movie in Korea called "집으로". Check that one out and you'll never forget this ending again. Until then:

신촌으로 갈까요? Should we go to Shin-chone? (Shin-chone is a college party area. Great for you young college kids! Not to be confused with 신천, which is on the other side of Seoul!)

우리집으로 와요. Come to my house.

앞으로 가세요. Go forward.

2 **못 V _can't V**

Our first way to say "can't." **못 V means can't V.**

A cautionary note: be sure to leave a space on both sides for all verbs—EXCEPT 하다! You can attach it to 하다.

A cautionary pronunciation note: When the 'ㅅ' 받침 comes before a 'ㅎ' on the next word, it goes from being pronounced [못] to being pronounced [모타다]. Be careful not to try to turn it into an 's' pronunciation.

In Korean you don't "go skiing" ~ you "ride skis." When people have trouble with that, they say:

스키를 못 타요.

And swimming is another sport that many have trouble with:

수영 못해요.

Though I'm one of the vertically challenged, so although I enjoy playing:

농구를 잘 못해요.

〉〉 Sentence Ending

1 V(으)세요(?)

Feel like you're having déjà vu? You've seen this before, but you don't quite know where? We originally learned this ending as a command/imperative form; a polite way to tell someone to do something. We're learning it again, but this time **V(으)세요 is a polite question (interrogative) ending or regular (declarative) sentence ending**. It's the equivalent of the first showing-respect method on page 111—V(으)시. The simple thing about this format is that you turn it into a question simply by raising your intonation. Now the taxi driver could have just said:

어디 가요?

That's okay, but it was much more polite for him to say:

어디 가세요?

At the end of a ride the taxi driver could say:

한국말을 잘 해요.

But he would be more polite if he said,

한국말을 잘 하세요.

This guy is really polite, isn't he?

2 V여/아/어 주다

Now it's your turn to be really polite. You could say, 가세요—the command form that we learned, but who likes to hear a command? Nobody, so let's end with something nicer. **V여/아/어 주다 means to do something for someone.** So when you want to ask someone to go somewhere, use:

가 주세요. (가+아=가—Don't forget.)

And when you want to ask someone to do you a favor, try:

해 주세요. (하+여=해—Don't forget.)

3 V네요!, N(이)네요! _Wow V, Wow N!

What we do with intonation in English, Koreans often have actual phrases for. I guess that's because there's a lot less intonation in the language to begin with. Anyway, "V네요." and "N(이)네요." **are endings that show surprise. This ending is not conjugated according to the** 받침. With the Korean you've already learned, you've probably heard this one a lot because Koreans are so surprised to hear a foreigner speak their language. There are so few foreigners in Korea that it still seems surprising to them. So you often hear:

한국말을 잘 하시네요!

If you and your friend see a beautiful woman, then you might say to your friend:

그 여자가 아름답네요!

You can use it with nouns too. Let's say you go to a Korean's house for dinner expecting them to serve rice and soup, but they serve pizza. Then you would say:

피자네요!

Understanding the Korean World

Understanding the taxis before you get to Korea is a good idea. They may look similar, but there are a lot of differences.

First of all there are the black taxis, otherwise known as 모범 택시 (deluxe taxis). They are over twice the price of regular taxis, but they have some advantages. First of all, they'll go anywhere in the nation at any time you get in. You can jump in a black taxi at two in the morning and go from Seoul to Pusan — an over 5-hour drive! And yes, it does happen. They are also larger and nicer cars than the regular taxis. Some of them are even mini-vans, but those are even more expensive.

Then there are two kinds of regular taxis that cost the same price: 회사 택시 with the blue light on top (Remember 회사원?) and 개인 택시 with the white light on top (private taxis). The company taxi drivers are usually under extreme pressure to make a lot of money, so if you want to get somewhere in a hurry, and you don't scare easy, go for it. If you prefer a safer, although perhaps less exciting ride, then go for the privately owned taxi drivers. They usually have many years of experience as well as more breathing space with their income since they don't have to pay the company owner part of their take.

Exercises

가 You're in a taxi. Try the following in Korean.

1. Tell the taxi driver to turn left.

2. Tell the taxi driver to turn right.

3. Tell the taxi driver to go straight.

나 Use the V(으)세요(?) ending to complete these sentences with the verbs given.

1. 어디 _____ ? (가다)

2. 뭘 _____ ? (공부하다)

3. _____ ? (춥다)

4. 운동을 정말 잘 _____ (하다)

다 Change this from a simple statement to a statement showing you're surprised (V네요).

1. 맛이 있어요. _____

2. 어려워요. _____

3. 배불러요. _____

4. 빨라요. _____

라 Tell me you can't do the following things.

1. 목욕탕에 가요. _____

2. 숙제를 해요. _____

3. 친구를 만나요. _____

마 Practice the following situation with a friend.

Imagine that you are in your hometown and you just left your favorite bar to head home. You get in the taxi and find that your taxi driver is Korean! (This actually happened to me in Las Vegas once, by the way.) Give him directions to your house in Korean!

CHAPTER 10

Stop please. I'm going to get out

세워 주세요. 내릴게요

"Where are you from?" It's one of the first questions you'll get as soon as you open your mouth and speak Korean. That's of course what our taxi driver is interested in as soon as he realizes he can communicate with this foreigner in Korea. You're going to hear "왔어요" a few times. That is the verb "to come" attached to the past tense ending making it "came." Of course we'll teach you more about this in a minute. You'll also hear John use one of the most common words in Korea—빨리. Koreans always seem to be in a hurry.

Dialog

택시 기사	어디에서 왔어요?
존	캐나다에서 왔어요.
택시 기사	캐나다에서 어떤 일을 했어요?
존	학생이었어요. 아저씨, 우리 집 다 왔어요. 세워 주세요. 내릴게요.
택시 기사	네, 이천육백 원 나왔어요.
존	빨리 왔네요. 고맙습니다.

Taxi driver Where from came?
John Canada from came.
Taxi driver Canada in what kind of work did?
John Student was. Mister, our house all came. Stop please. I'll get out.
Taxi driver Yes. Two thousand six hundred won came out.
John Quickly came wow. Thank you.

Taxi driver	Where are you from?
John	I'm from Canada.
Taxi driver	What did you do in Canada?
John	I was a student. Mister, my house is right here. Stop please. I'll get out.
Taxi driver	Sure. That'll be 2,600 won.
John	We got here fast. Thanks.

Key Expressions

N에서 왔어요. I'm from N. (오다—오 + 았 + 어요)

세워 주세요. Please stop (the vehicle).

내릴게요. I'd like to get out.

~원 나왔어요. That comes to ~ won.

여기 있어요. Here you go.

였/았/었어요 past tense modifier

어떤 what kind of

학생 student

우리 our

다 all

내리다 to get off/out (of a vehicle)

빨리 quickly

캐나다 Canada

일 work

아저씨 greeting for an older man

집 house

세우다 to stop (a vehicle)

나오다 to come out

Bonus Vocabulary

택시를 탈 때 When you ride a taxi

(택시) 기사 driver
승객 passenger
택시비 taxi expense
손님 customer
택시 요금 taxi fare

택시 관련 동사 Taxi-related verbs

타다 to ride
계속 가다 to continue to go
세우다 to stop (transitive form)
내리다 to get out, to get off
잠깐 멈추다 to stop for a moment
(값이) 나오다 to come to a price

속도 부사 Speed adverbs

빨리 quickly
천천히 slowly

오디오와 비디오 Audio and video

라디오 radio
비디오 video
카세트 cassette
텔레비전 television
디비디 DVD

Getting It

>> **Sentence Ending**

1 V였/았/었어요

I'm sure you remember the "V여/아/어요" conjugation for present tense. This works exactly the same way, only you add the 쌍 시옷 (ㅆ) at the end. This is one of the most commonly used grammar patterns you have seen so far. Use "V였/았/었어요." **to make past tense sentences**. Practice using this until it becomes habit. One of the most confusing but common mistakes of beginning learners is the use of the wrong tense. It takes a lot of practice to get right. Did you practice?

안 했어요.

Then do it before you read another word. Did you do it?

했어요. (하 + 였 = 하였 = 했)

Good, glad to hear it. Now go out and use it with a Korean friend right now and come back. Did you come back yet?

왔어요. (오 + 았 = 왔)

Nice job. You must be famished. Go get yourself something to eat now.

먹었어요.

Oh. You ate? In that case, you'd better move on to the next topic.

2 V(으)ㄹ게요 _ I'll V

Remember those endings that we would accomplish with intonation in English? Here's another one. We might say something in a slightly higher tone in order to ask permission for something, but in Korean you just use this ending. "V(으)ㄹ게요." **shows your intention to do something if the other person has no objections**. It is common when you're sitting down to eat and someone else is treating or has cooked. You tell them you'll enjoy the food they have kindly served or purchased by eating well:

잘 먹을게요.

Or when someone is buying the beer you could use:

잘 마실게요.

When you've had enough to drink and eat and you think it's time to go it's nice to see if anyone has any objections by telling them:

갈게요.

Actually I'm tired of writing Chapter 10 and I'm hungry too. Sorry folks but

밥 먹으러 갈게요!

〉〉 Auxiliary

V(으)러 가다/오다 _ to go (or come) somewhere in order to V

Notice this one always starts with a verb. Use **V(으)러 가다/오다 to give your reason (verb only) for going (or coming) somewhere**. Make sure not to confuse it with the one that gets the noun. That one is for giving directions, right? N(으)로 is a totally different auxiliary. Why are you going to the store later?

우유를 사러 가요. (Notice that simple present tense can apply to the future as well.*)

And why are you in the library right now?

공부하러 왔어요.

And why do people go to restaurants?

밥 먹으러 가요.

★ In English we use progressive tense to refer to future: I'm working tomorrow. This doesn't work in Korean.

Understanding the Korean World

Asia is always said to be more community-focused while the West is more individualistic, and it comes through in the Korean language as well. The concept of "we" and "us" permeates the Korean language and society.

It's not called "my" country, its 우리 나라. It's not my house, its 우리 집 even if you live alone! It's not "my" family, it's 우리 가족 and often it's not 한국말, it's 우리말. It may seem even stranger that it's not "my" mom or "my" dad, but 우리 엄마 and 우리 아빠. But, you know, I can understand those since you could have brothers and sisters to share them with. The thing that seems really strange to me is that sometimes they start referring to their husband as 우리 남편 and wife as 우리 아내. Who are they sharing them with?

The language aside, becoming part of the same group makes you part of the same "우리" and until you're the same "우리" you really are often disregarded. But find a way to make it into someone's "우리" and you are family for life. It could be graduating from the same school ~ 우리 학교. Or working for the same company ~ 우리 회사. It could be having the same last name. It could be being the same age, having the same hometown or having lived in the same area ~ most of these being difficult for a Korean newcomer to achieve. All of these things, however, will set into motion the instant friendship that comes from being part of the same "우리."

Exercises

가 Make the following sentences past tense.

1. 해요. _____

2. 봐요. _____

3. 와요. _____

4. 읽어요. _____

나 Tell why you go to these places.

1. 식당

_____

2. 슈퍼

_____

3. 도서관

_____

다 Politely tell someone you're going to do the following.

1. 오늘 밤에 전화해요.

   _____

2. 내일 일찍 와요.

   _____

3. 한국말을 열심히 공부해요.

   _____

4. 조금 이따가 가요.

   _____

라 Practice the following situation with a friend.

You just bumped into that elementary school crush that you had when you were young. He (she) is just as attractive as when you were little kids, and it turns out that he (she) is fluent in Korean too. Try catching up by telling him (her) what you have been up to over the last few years (or decades, as in my case may be).

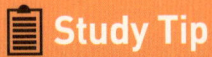

Study Tip

Koreans Aren't Always Right!

You know very well that there are people who speak your native language better than others. There are many common mistakes even native speakers of English make, like using "good" as an adverb; you don't do it "good," you do it "well." There are some common mistakes Koreans often make that could confuse you, so I'm here to clear them up. You'll also score a lot of points with people if you can point out the mistakes that even native Korean speakers make.

1) "가르치다" means "to teach" and "가리키다" means "to point / to point out." Often Koreans will confuse them and use "가르키다" for "to teach." Remember the difference.

2) "너무" means "too" — too much or too many, or as we hear, "too spicy." It's supposed to be used when something is excessive, but nowadays it is very common for people to use it for emphasis, as in, "너무 예뻐요." Try not to develop this habit, because sometimes it can be confusing to the listener.

3) "다르다" means "to be different," and "틀리다" means "to be wrong." Again the difference is becoming blurred. Sometimes people will say something is wrong, when they really mean that it is different. Don't copy this mistake!

4) Trust me, I'm not lying. When the previous vowel is an "ㅏ" you add 아요 to the verb stem. You'll constantly hear Koreans pronounce "바빠요" as "바뻐", "아파요" as "아퍼" or "같아요" as "같애". Don't be fooled by this deception! They're trying to make you speak and write bad Korean!

5) Just like the pronunciation error in number four, you'll frequently hear the vowel "오" pronounced like an "우". They're at it again! "Me too" in the low form is "나도" NOT "나두". "What did you say?" is "뭐라고요?" NOT "뭐라구요?"

CHAPTER 11
It's me. Who is this?
전데요. 누구세요?

John made it home and got in a good night's sleep in his new abode. He slept in late, jet lag being a factor. After waking up, having a big breakfast and his morning coffee, he sat down to read the morning paper. About halfway through the Opinion (오피니언) section, the phone rings. Who could it be? Of course it's Yoo-shik calling to see what John is up to.

It turns out that 유식 is 심심해요 (bored). Or maybe being the nice guy that he is, 유식 doesn't want John to think that he is simply concerned about him. Regardless, he invites John to go shopping or grab a meal. But John just feels like seeing a movie.

Dialog

존	여보세요?
유식	존 씨 좀 바꿔 주시겠어요?
존	네. 전데요. 누구세요?
유식	유식이에요. 지금 뭐 하고 있어요?
존	신문을 보고 있어요. 유식 씨는 뭐 해요?
유식	심심해요. 우리 오늘 쇼핑이나 식사할까요?
존	그냥 영화를 봅시다.
유식	그렇게 합시다.

John Hello?
Yoo-shik John Mr. change for me please would?
John Yes. John. Who please?
Yoo-shik Yoo-shik is. Now what are doing?
John Paper am looking. Yoo-shik what do?
Yoo-shik Bored. We today shopping or meal do shall?
John Just movie see let's.
Yoo-shik Like that do let's.

John	Hello?
Yoo-shik	Could I please speak to John?
John	Sure. This is John. Who is calling please?
Yoo-shik	This is Yoo-shik. What are you doing right now?
John	I'm just reading the paper. What are you up to?
Yoo-shik	I'm bored. How about going shopping or grabbing a bite to eat?
John	Let's just see a movie.
Yoo-shik	Okay, let's do that.

Key Expressions

여보세요? Hello? ("여보세요" is used only when answering the telephone or trying to get someone's attention.)

누구세요? Who is it, please? / Who is this, please?

P 좀 바꿔 주시겠어요? Could I please speak to P?*

전데요.(저인데요.) It's me, what can I do for you?

뭐 하고 있어요? What are you doing?

뭐 해요? What are you doing?

심심해요. I'm bored.

그렇게 합시다. Let's do that.

좀 please
바꾸다 to change
은/는데요 polite sentence ending asking for more information
누구 Who
V고 있다 to be doing V (present continuous tense)
그냥 just, just because
신문 newspaper
심심하다 to be bored
오늘 today
쇼핑 shopping
N(이)나 N N or N
식사 food, a meal
V(으)ㅂ시다 Let's V.
그렇게 like that

★ P=person

Bonus Vocabulary

전화하기 Calling

바꾸다 to change (to turn the phone over to someone else)
잠깐 one moment
통화중이다 to be busy, to be in the middle of a call
(전화) 잘못 걸다 to dial a wrong number

놀 거리 Things to do for fun

관광 sightseeing　　쇼핑 shopping　　공연 a performance
전시회 an exhibition　　연극 a play　　뮤지컬 a musical
오페라 an opera　　콘서트 a concert　　음악회 a concert

언제 When

어제 yesterday　　오늘 today　　내일 tomorrow
지난주 last week　　이번 주 this week　　다음 주 next week
지난달 last month　　이번 달 this month　　다음 달 next month
작년 last year　　올해 this year　　내년 next year

Getting It

〉〉 Sentence Ending

1 N인데요, A(으)ㄴ데요, V는데요

You've already had the word "그런데," and you learned that it means "but." That is often true, but it can also have other meanings and forms. Conjunctions in Korean can usually end a sentence as well; you just add "요" to the end to be polite. They usually mean the same thing as when they are conjunctions, but in this case, it's a little different. When "~ㄴ데요" is used at the end of a sentence, not in the beginning or middle, the intonation will usually go up. That is because "**N인데요, A(으)ㄴ데요, V는데요**" **ending requests more information or comment.** In the dialog when John says, "It's me," with this ending, he is showing that he would like to hear who is on the other end of the line, and/or what it is concerning.

Let's say your boss calls and says to come over right away, but you don't know why he asked you to come. You would arrive and say,

왔는데요. I came (so what's up?).

And how about if your friend asks you if you have money, and you're curious why she is asking:

없는데요. I don't have any (but what do you need it for?).

Of course you're not going to admit you have money, right? That's just asking for trouble.

2 V고 있다 _to be Ving

Now I hope that you noticed that there the basic "V여/아/어요" ending is quite often used for present progressive tense. In English, when something is in the process of happening, we are pretty strict about using the present progressive tense, but not in this language. You can use simple present tense to talk about an action in progress more often, but you still have to know how to say the progressive tense. Good news—no conjugation necessary! **V고 있다 is used for actions in progress**.

You are eating, and your friend calls and asks, "What are you doing?"

먹고 있어요. I'm eating.

Who are you eating with? You're not alone, are you? (Koreans always feel sorry for anyone who has to eat alone.)

친구를 만나고 있어요.

That's a relief. I was afraid you were alone. Let's get real now. Tell me what you are really doing right now:

한국말을 공부하고 있어요.

That's right, and you're doing a great job. Chapter 11 is probably farther than most people get. Maintain the pace and listen to the tape every day!

3 V(으)ㅂ시다   _Let's V.

John has another idea about what they should do, doesn't he? So he says, "Let's just see a movie." How did he do that? He added "to see" (보다) to the sentence ending ㅂ시다 (One advantage of Korean is there is only one word for "to look," "to watch," as well as "to see."). The result is 보 + ㅂ시다 = 봅시다. "**V(으)ㅂ시다**" **tells someone you want to do something together.**

We're sticking with the food examples to start.

You're with your friend and you're getting hungry. Suggest some lunch:

밥 먹읍시다.   Let's eat lunch. (Remember rice can mean "food" as well.)

You go to a restaurant; you and your friend both know what you want, so it's time to order. Tell your friend:

주문합시다.

Now that you've done that, it's time to go get some drink:

커피나 차 한잔 합시다.

》 Conjunction

N(이)나 N _N or N

Pizza or 비빔밥? Tuesday or Thursday? 5:15 or 5:50? N(이)나 N **is used offer a choice between two things.**
Let's try the first example above ~

피자나 비빔밥 먹을까요?

All my examples seem to do with eating, don't they? Let's try something different this time. You want to go to the mountains this weekend, and you don't care which day you go:

토요일이나 일요일에 산에 가고 싶어요.

And in Korea, after you have your meal, they often include something to drink or a dessert afterward. It's called 후식. So after the meal the waitress may offer you something like this:

(후식으로는) 아이스크림이나 차 있어요.

I just can't seem to get away from these food examples, I guess.

Understanding the Korean World

In Korea, there is an incredibly important concept that you must understand in order to know how to behave and what others will expect of you. It is all summed up in one single word: 눈치. 눈치 can roughly be translated to, "sensibilities" or "perceptiveness." Dealing with rejection is one instance in which 눈치 is very necessary. In many countries when you don't want to do something, you just say you're not interested. In Korean that is considered impolite, so it is more common to make excuses about why you can't do something. When you hear people making excuses about why they can't do something, you should understand that often they really just don't want to do it, but they don't want to come out and say it. So don't try to figure out a way around their excuses; they'll say that you don't have 눈치.

It also works the other way around. One of the funniest things in Korea to me is trying to offer food. If you've got a snack and you offer it to a Korean, they ALWAYS reject the first offer. If they rejected abruptly without even looking at it, then they probably really don't want any. But if they look at it, pause and then reject hesitantly, then they really want some, but they don't want to take any in case you just offered to be polite. But you're rude if you don't offer again! Usually it's a good idea to offer at least three times. But you may not have to if you have 눈치. You can tell on your own what they are thinking. It's kind of like mind reading, only a little harder.

Exercises

가 Show that you don't agree and don't quite understand why they're asking using V는데요.

1. 맛이 없죠?

2. 지난 달에 공부 안 했죠?

3. 친구를 못 만났죠?

나 Combine the following into a single sentence with two choices.

1. 금요일에 가요? 토요일에 가요?

   _____

2. 불고기를 먹을까요? 갈비를 먹을까요?

   _____

3. 여섯 시에 만날까요? 일곱 시에 만날까요?

   _____

다 Invite someone to do the following with you.

1. 커피숍에서 이야기해요.

   _____

2. 쉬어요.

   _____

3. 닭갈비를 먹어요.

   _____

4. 지하철을 타요.

   _____

5. 집에서 책을 읽어요.

   _____

라 Practice the following situation with a friend.

Unbelievable! Your favorite musicians, The Backstreet Boys, are coming to your city to play in concert! Call your friend and invite her (him) to join you for the concert.

CHAPTER 12
I get it. See you a little later
알았어요. 이따 봐요

John and Yoo-shik are all set to see a movie, but now John needs to figure out how to get to the movie theater. The theater is in 명동, a trendy area not too far from 남대문, which is filled with tourists and young Koreans looking for the next fashion craze. John wants to know if he can ride the bus, but as is typical in Korea, Yoo-shik says that the subway is faster. The word 지하 means underground, and 철 is the Sino-Korean word for steel, and combined they mean metro/subway—지하철. Yoo-shik gives John directions. He has to ride line six and then transfer to line number four at 삼각지 station. Fearing a long ride, John asks if it is far after the transfer, but Yoo-shik reassures him that he only has to go four stops. John understands and ends the conversation with, "See you in a bit."

Dialog

존	명동에 어떻게 가요? 버스로 갈 수 있어요?
유식	지하철을 타면 더 빨라요.
존	지하철로 어떻게 가요?
유식	상수역에서 6호선을 타세요. 그리고 삼각지역에서 4호선으로 갈아타야 돼요.
존	삼각지역에서 멀어요?
유식	아니오. 네 정거장만 가면 돼요.
존	알았어요. 이따 봐요.

John 명동 to how go? Bus by go can?
Yoo-shik Subway ride if more fast.
John Subway by how go?
Yoo-shik 상수 station at line 6 ride. And 삼각지 station at line 4 to transfer have to.
John 삼각지 station from far?
Yoo-shik No. Four stops only go if done.
John Knew. A little later see.

John	How do I get to 명동? Can I go by bus?
Yoo-shik	It's faster if you ride the subway.
John	How do I get there by subway?
Yoo-shik	Ride line 6 at 상수 station. Then you have to transfer to line 4 at 삼각지 station.
John	Is it far from 삼각지 station?
Yoo-shik	No. Just go four stops and you're there.
John	I get it. See you in a bit.

Key Expressions

P에 어떻게 가요? How do I get to P?*

T(으)로 어떻게 가요? How do I get there by T?*

지하철을 타면 더 빨라요. It's faster if you ride the subway.

~호선으로 갈아타세요. Transfer to line ~.

여기에서 멀어요? Is it far from here?

~ 정거장만 가면 돼요. Just go ~ stops.

알았어요. I see., I get it.

이따 봐요. See you later. ("이따" is short for "이따가", which you may remember from chapter 6, means "a little later." Don't get it confused with the verb "있다".)

어떻게 How
버스 bus
V(으)ㄹ 수 있다 can

지하철 subway
더 A/V more A/V*
역 station

호선 line
갈아타다 to transfer

멀다 to be far (a regular verb, NOT an irregular "ㄹ" verb)

정거장 stops (bus or subway)

되다 to be enough (the verb 되다 has more meanings than a Milan Kundera novel. If you look it up in a Korean-English dictionary you'll spend a few pages trying to figure out which one is appropriate. In this instance, it would be "to be enough.")

알다 to know
이따 a short while later

★ P=place, T=mode of transportation, A/V=adjective/verb

Bonus Vocabulary

얼마나 걸려요? How long does it take?

가깝다 to be nearby
가까운 near (noun modifying adjective—가까운 곳)
멀다 to be far
먼 far (noun modifying adjective—먼 곳)

오고 가다 Coming and going

도착 arrival
출발 departure
도착하다 to arrive
출발하다 to depart

지하철 역에서 At the subway station

매표소 ticket booth
계단 stairs
안전선 safety line
에스컬레이터 escalator
선로 train tracks
엘리베이터 elevator

서울 지하철 노선 Seoul subway lines

1호선 The dark-blue line
3호선 The orange line
5호선 The purple line
7호선 The olive line
2호선 The green line
4호선 The light-blue line
6호선 The light-brown line
8호선 The pink line

Getting It

>> **Sentence Ending**

1 V(으)ㄹ 수 있다, V(으)ㄹ 수 없다 _can, can't

Here is how you talk about possibility. Isn't it interesting how "있다, 없다" are used to show possibility? With a little work this one is pretty easy to pick up. We've had the "(으)ㄹ" format quite a few times already, and you're familiar with "있다, 없다," so now all you really need to do is add "수" in between. (Make sure you put a space on both sides.) "V(으)ㄹ 수 있다" **expresses the ability to V and** "V(으)ㄹ 수 없다" **expresses the inability to V.** One thing to keep in mind is that this is not used to ask permission!

One of the strangest questions you may hear has to do with eating (who would have guessed?). People will often ask you:

김치 먹을 수 있어요? Do you eat kimchi?

That's right. If you hear this question, it has less to do with possibility and more to do with your preferences. Of course you can physically eat it (although some have been known to lack this ability), but what they're really asking is if you eat it regularly. You'll hear the same question about spicy food.

매운 거 먹을 수 있어요?

Another one you'll hear a lot if you look foreign, of course, is:

한국말 할 수 있어요?

And your response at this point would have to be:

네, 할 수 있어요.

But let's just say you aren't in the mood to the person, so you're going to pretend you can't:

아니요, 한국말을 할 수 없어요.

거짓말쟁이! Liar!

2 V여/아/어야 되다 _to have to V

We all have times when there is something we have no choice but to do. When that time comes we say we "have to" do it. "**V여/아/어야 되다**" **means one "must V"**. You've arrived in Korea, and you're going to spend some time here, then you'd better learn Korean:

한국말을 배워야 돼요.

Then it's a good idea to get out of the house, and go meet your language exchange partner, even if you would like to stay in.

나가야 돼요. (Remember 나오다 was "to come out" and 나가다 is "to go out".)

And you can't just do exchanges. If you really want to become good at conversational Korean, what is the key?

이야기를 많이 해야 돼요.

That's right, so even if the conversation is a little hard to follow, keep listening and trying!

》 Conjunction

V(으)면 _If V

Once again you have to flip it around. The verb stem comes before the word for "if", but it's the same meaning. "**V(으)면**" **is used for conditional statements**— "If V."

Let's say you're going shopping this time. But you don't have much money and your friend wants to go shopping at an expensive department store:

비싸면 안 사요. If it's expensive, I'm not buying.

Your friend understands this, but tells you there's a sale, and when there's a sale the department stores are good deals. Now you want to tell your friend you'll buy:

안 비싸면 살게요. If it's not expensive I'll buy (something).

Now you want to introduce your friend to a girl, but before you do you want to know what kind of girl he likes. You ask him what kind of girl would be okay, and he has a very simple answer:

예쁘면 돼요. If she's pretty, that's enough.

》 Auxiliary

더 A _more A, Aer

Here's an easy one. Simply put 더 in front of an adjective in the same way we use "more" or when we add "er" to an adjective.

How would you say this one is bigger?

이것이 더 커요.

How about that one is cheaper?

그것이 더 싸요.

Or ask if that one tastes better?

그것이 더 맛있어요?

Not too challenging, is it?

Understanding the Korean World

    Korean cities probably have some of the best subways in the world. They are clean, dirt cheap, reliable, safe, and best of all the seats usually have cushions! (Although I've noticed some of the lines are doing away with the cushions, which really scares me.) One of the things that makes it so easy to use the subway is those bright colors that they use for the lines, and people new to Seoul always use colors to talk about the different subway lines: the green line, the orange line, etc. This includes people from other parts of Korea who don't know the subway lines well. But everyone who spends time in Seoul has to start learning the line numbers and using the numbers instead of the colors. Why would this be? I've given this a lot of thought, and I think I've figured it out. The lines were built one at a time (when I originally came in 1995 they had only completed the first four lines), so when they had one line, it was just "the subway line." But then they added another line, and for quite a few years it was the 일호선 and 이호선. Now the subway map looks like a crazy rainbow, but they still use the numbers, just like the old days.

Exercises

가 Tell me you can do the following.

1. 냉면을 먹다.

2. 한국말을 하다.

3. 화요일에 만나다.

나 Tell me you cannot do the following.

1. 술을 마시다.

2. 지금 나가다.

3. 중국어를 하다.

다 Use V(으)면 to show that the second statement is dependent on the first.

1. 한국말을 잘 해요. 한국이 더 재미있어요.

   _____

2. 기차를 타요. 더 빨라요.

   _____

3. 숙제를 해요. 많이 배워요.

   _____

라 Tell me you have no choice but to do the following.

1. 숙제를 하다. _____

2. 5호선을 타다. _____

3. 한글을 배우다. _____

마 Practice the following situation with a friend.

Get yourself a map of the Seoul subway system. You need to go from 홍대입구역 to 압구정역. Ask your friend how to get there and make sure to write down the directions.

CHAPTER 13 죄송합니다, 손님
Sorry, customer

유식 and John have arrived in front of the movie theater now. John knows that 유식 saw a movie last week at the same place, and he asks about how the movie was. 유식 says he enjoyed the movie and then their attention turns to more urgent matters—the movie they're going to watch today. John asks 유식 if he "예매했어요?" (reserved tickets in advance), as is often necessary at Korean theaters due to the crowds. It turns out that he couldn't, so they have to pick up their tickets now. Sure enough, the next showing 매진됐어요 (was sold out), but there are tickets to a later showing, which they quickly snatch up.

Dialog

존	지난주에 본 영화 어땠어요?
유식	재미있었어요.
존	그래요? 그런데 오늘 볼 영화 예매했어요?
유식	아니요, 못했어요. 지금 표 사야 돼요.
	(잠시 후)
유식	〈집으로〉 두 장 주시겠어요?
직원	죄송합니다, 손님. 4시 20분 것은 매진됐는데 6시 45분 것으로 보시겠어요?
유식	그래요. 6시 45분 것으로 할게요.

John Last week at seen movie how was?
Yoo-shik Fun had.
John Really? And today see will movie reserved?
Yoo-shik No, couldn't. Now buy ticket have to.
(moment after)
Yoo-shik 〈집으로〉 two tickets give could you please?
Clerk Sorry, customer. 4 o'clock 20 minute one sold out however 6 o'clock 45 minute one see would like?
Yoo-shik Sure. 6 o'clock 45 minute one do will.

John How was the movie you saw last week?
Yoo-shik It was pretty good.
John Really? And did you reserve tickets for today's movie?
Yoo-shik No, I couldn't. We have to get them now.
(after a moment)
Yoo-shik Two tickets for <집으로> please.
Clerk Sorry, but the 4:20 showing is sold out. Would you like to see the 6:45 showing?
Yoo-shik Sure, I'll take the 6:45 showing.

Key Expressions

영화가 어땠어요? How was the movie?

재미있었어요. It was good., It was fun.

그래요? Really?

예매했어요? Did you reserve tickets?

못했어요. I couldn't.

N(을/를) 사야 돼요. I have to buy N.

죄송합니다. I'm sorry.

지난 past, last
(으)ㄴ past verb ending
예매하다 to reserve tickets
죄송하다 to be sorry

주 week
오늘 today
장 counter for paper
매진되다 to be sold out

➕ Bonus Vocabulary

비평 Critique

재미있다 to be fun (to be good/great)
재미없다 to be no fun (to be boring)
감동적이다 to be moving, impressive
지루하다 to be boring
형편없다 to be terrible/worthless/dreadful

영화 장르 Movie genre

드라마 a drama
액션 영화 an action movie
SF(에스에프) 영화 a science fiction movie
코믹 영화 a comedy movie
공포 영화 a horror movie

단위 명사 Counters

개 counter for everything without another specified counter (사과 한 개)
장 counter for pieces of paper (표 다섯 장)
잔 cup (물 두 잔)
병 bottle (맥주 세 병)
명 counter for people (여자 네 명)
분 counter for people (honorific—선생님 두 분)

문구 School/office supplies

종이 paper
펜 pen
연필 pencil
지우개 eraser

Getting It

〉〉 Auxiliary

N(으)로 주세요., N(으)로 할게요. _Please give me N., I'll take N.

I know we've had it before, but it's a little different this time. It can be used for destinations, but this time it is used for a choice that you make. "**N(으)로**" is used when one chooses N.

You saw a few examples in the dialog. Now I'm going to combine some practice with review here. Remember how to turn a sentence-ending adjective into a noun-modifying adjective? Right! You simply add ㄴ/은. Let's pick out a few things using some adjectives that we know.

I'll take the small one, please:

작은 것으로 주세요.

Now you're ordering coffee and you'd like the big cup:

큰 잔으로 주시겠어요? (a more polite request)

And now for a usage that will throw you a little, I'll take the cheap bicycle:

싼 자전거로 할게요.

Yes, in colloquial English we may say that we'll "take" it when we want to buy something, but Koreans say that they'll "do" it in colloquial Korean.

〉〉 Conjunction

N인데, A(으)ㄴ데, V는데 _and, but, in spite of, etc.

Sometimes it may seem like Koreans use conjunctions with every sentence when you hear them speaking. This is the most common conjunction, probably because it can have the most meanings. N인데, A은데, V는데 is used to connect two related ideas. It can be the equivalent of but, and, in spite of, etc. Sometimes the parts might even seem unrelated, but they may just be on the same topic.

Let's say you want to tell someone you left your money at home:

집에 돈이 있는데 지금은 없어요. (Notice that 있다 and 없다 are treated like regular verbs in this format.)

What if the clothes are pretty, but they're too expensive:

예쁜데 너무 비싸요.

And now you're tired and want to take a rest.

피곤한데 쉽시다!

〉〉 Korean Key

Making a verb into an adjective

V ㄴ   past tense V

V 는   present tense V

V(으)ㄹ   future tense V

How do you make a verb into an adjective? In English you can't do it. You need a whole clause to show the relationship; 'the movie that I saw', 'the person who I met', 'the company I work at', 'the clothes that I will wear'. Not so in Korean. With Korean we can just add a letter or two to the end of a verb and it is transformed into an adjective right before your very eyes ~ like magic!

만난 사람

입을 옷

다니는 회사 (Don't forget that you "attend" a company as well as a school in Korean!)

It's like magic, isn't it? Try being a magician yourself and making a few verbs into adjectives that can describe nouns in your spare time.

Understanding the Korean World

A few things may surprise you about trips to the movie theaters in Korea. The first I've already alluded to: they're incredibly crowded. You might as well forget about seeing a movie if you don't have tickets at least an hour before the show on weekends. It's probably sold out already. The next surprise is likely to be "Korean popcorn": dried squid. Women especially love this snack which has a bit of an aroma to it. Nowadays popcorn has become popular enough to overcome the scent for the most part, but you may want to get your own box of popcorn to ensure your own defense. Finally, and most annoying is that sometimes a cell phone may ring, be answered, and sometimes a conversation may even ensue in the seat next to you. This annoys most Koreans as well, but in general Koreans try to avoid conflict and prefer to let small things slide. Often a dirty look will do the trick, but I don't make any guarantees. Again, technology may solve this problem as many theaters are installing cell phone scramblers to stop these offenders before they even get started.

Exercises

가 Politely request the following (end with "V시겠어요?").

1. three sheets of paper

   | | | | | | | | | | | ?

2. four bottles of beer

   | | | | | | | | | | | ?

3. two glasses of wine

   | | | | | | | | | | | ?

나 Tell them your choice.

1. I'll take the white one.

   | | | | | | | | |

2. Please give me the small one.

   | | | | | | | | |

3. I'll take a seat in the front.

   | | | | | | |

다 Combine the two sentences with ~는데.

1. 하얀색은 있어요. 검은색이 없어요.

   _____

2. 어려워요. 할 수 있어요.

   _____

3. 숙제를 했어요. 이해할 수 없어요.

   _____

4. 주스는 있어요. 술이 없어요.

   _____

라 Practice the following situation with a friend.

It's time to do some shopping. You're at the 백화점 doing some shopping. The clerk is out of what you are looking for, but he/she offers some alternatives. Choose amongst one of those.

CHAPTER 14
Spring will come soon
봄이 금방 올 거예요

John has been in Korea for a few weeks now, and he's really enjoying himself in the new country that he calls home. One thing is starting to bother him, however. He arrived at a very cold time of the year and he's starting to get tired of being cold all the time. He asks 유식 about the weather in February, hoping to hear that it will warm up a little. No such luck. 추워요 (Cold) says 유식. The forecast calls for cold weather and more snow. John's not too happy about this situation as he hates cold weather. Yoo-shik urges him to 기다려요 (wait). He reassures him that spring is on the way. That doesn't help John much, who apparently isn't so good at waiting. He asks if there isn't some warm place in Korea.

존	너무 추워요. 한국의 2월 날씨는 어때요?
유식	추워요. 눈도 올 거예요.
존	정말이요? 전 추운 날씨가 싫어요.
유식	조금만 기다려요. 봄이 금방 올 거예요.
존	기다리기도 싫어요. 한국에 따뜻한 곳은 없어요?

John Too cold. Korea 2 month weather how is?
Yoo-shik Cold. Snow too come going to.
John Really? I cold weather hate.
Yoo-shik A little only wait. Spring soon come going to.
John Waiting too hate. Korea warm place not have?

John	It's too cold. How is the weather in Korea in February?
Yoo-shik	It's cold. It's going to snow too.
John	Really? I hate cold weather.
Yoo-shik	Wait a little while. Spring is going to come soon.
John	I hate waiting too. Isn't there a warm place in Korea?

Key Expressions

너무 추워요. It's too cold.

눈이 올 거예요. It's going to snow.

N이/가 싫어요. I don't like N., I hate N.

V기 싫어요. I don't want to V., I hate Ving.

조금만 기다려요. Just wait a little bit.

N이/가 금방 올 거예요. N will come soon.

월 month
날씨 weather
(으)ㄹ 거예요 to be going to
조금 a little
따뜻하다 to be warm

춥다 to be cold (air temperature)
어떻다 how
눈 snow
기다리다 to wait
봄 spring

금방 near the present time (It means both "soon" and "a short time ago.")

곳 place

Bonus Vocabulary

온도 Temperature

춥다 to be cold (air temperature)
추운 cold (noun modifier—추운 날씨)
쌀쌀하다 to be chilly   쌀쌀한 chilly (noun modifier—쌀쌀한 날씨)
시원하다 to be cool   시원한 cool (noun modifier—시원한 날씨)
덥다 to be hot   더운 hot (noun modifier—더운 날씨)
따뜻하다 to be warm   따뜻한 warm (noun modifier—따뜻한 날씨)

계절 Seasons

봄 spring   여름 summer   가을 fall   겨울 winter

몇 월? What month? (Notice the two pronunciation exceptions!)

1월 January   2월 February   3월 March
4월 April   5월 May   6월 June [유월]
7월 July   8월 August   9월 September
10월 October [시월]   11월 November   12월 December

Getting It

〉〉 Sentence Ending

A/V(으)ㄹ 거예요

I always consider the difference between "A/V겠어요" and "A/V을 거예요" similar to the difference between "will" and "be going to" in English. Both are **used in giving predictions about the future, and both are used for expressing intention.** For now, consider "겠" to be the slightly more formal (and commonly written) one, while (으)ㄹ 거예요 is used more often in spoken, less formal circumstances.

So before we go on, let's go over the weather you can expect in Korea during each season. How will it be in spring?

봄은 따뜻할 거예요.

And in the summer?

여름은 더울 거예요.

That's right. The humidity is a bear. Now what can we expect in the fall?

가을은 쌀쌀할 거예요.

It starts to get chilly around October. And in winter, as Yoo-shik already pointed out:

겨울은 추울 거예요.

My Canadian friends sometimes tell me how Korea doesn't have very cold winters. That's why you'll never see me in Canada in the winter.

추우니까 안 갈 거예요.

〉〉 Contraction

verbs ending in "ㅣ"

Here's another contraction that is so common that you'll never see the full form. **Verbs that end in the vowel "ㅣ" when conjugated with the "ㅓ요" form become "ㅕ요".** Originally the verb "to wait" should be conjugated like this, right?

기다리 + 어요 = 기다리어요.

But if you say three times quickly, then you may notice that the vowels blend together until you're pronouncing it kind of like this:

기다려요.

Another verb that you know which ends in "ㅣ" is 걸리다. Ask how long it takes:

얼마나 걸려요?

And finally, you know "to get out" of a car, bus, etc. Try saying I get off at 강남역.

강남역에서 내려요.

〉〉 Korean Key

Double Subjects

One of the most astounding things to an English speaker is that you can have two subjects in one sentence. You do that by using both the contrastive/topic marker 은/는 and the subject marker 이/가. For me, the most representative double subject sentence is one you will see in Korean dramas and soap operas every time the man admits his love to the woman he is pursuing:

나는 네가 좋아.

"나" is "I" in the casual form. "너" is the casual form for "you", and when the subject marker "가" is attached it changes to "네", which is usually pronounced "니가" in spoken Korean. If you take off the "요" ending, then you get the common casual form sentence ending.

You see how Koreans use themselves as the topic of the sentence, but the thing that is "good" is the young lady they are pursuing. They themselves are simply the conduit of that feeling. It's the same with today's dialog:

저는 추운 날씨가 싫어요.

John hates cold weather, and since he is talking about his feelings, it is one of the common sentences for the double subject.

제가 김치를 좋아해요.

Easy, huh? Subject, object, verb. Well let's say you wanted to do this with a double subject. How would it be different?

저는 김치가 좋아요.

〉〉 Auxiliary

V기 _Ving

We use verbs as subjects in English all the time, but to do it we usually add "ing" to the end. Waiting is no fun, is it? **Add 기 to the end of a verb to make it the noun form.**

걷기가 정말 좋아요.

Exercises is catching on in Korea, but you will still find many people who don't enjoy it:

운동하기가 힘들어요.

Okay, I don't know your opinion of exercise but I bet I know how you feel about speaking Korean:

한국말 하기가 재미있어요.

I'm glad to hear it (whether it's true or not).

Understanding the Korean World

The weather isn't the only thing that changes with the seasons in Korea. There are specific foods that only show up when the season is right. In the winter on the side of the street you can find the vendors selling 군밤 (roasted chestnuts)—a great healthy snack. Winter also brings out the 붕어빵—goldfish bread. It is made from a pancake batter and has sweet red bean in the middle—great snack on cold days. "붕어빵" has also come to mean "twins" or "to look exactly alike" since all fish look exactly alike straight out of the mold.

Summer of course brings cooler foods. One popular snack is also made with the sweetened red beans—팥빙수. "팥" actually refers to the red beans and 빙수 is Sino-Korean and means "frozen water," in this case shaved ice. It usually has cream or ice cream in it too. Nowadays most places also serve 과일빙수—fruit shaved ice. Summer also brings a cold buckwheat noodle called 냉면. 냉 means cold and 면 means noodle. The noodles are served with your choice of a cold beef broth or a spicy red sauce. Either way it's a healthy refreshing dish to get on a hot summer day.

Exercises

가 Change the following sentences to future tense—(으)ㄹ 거예요.

1. 아침에 샤워해요.
   내일 아침에 _____

2. 여름은 더워요.
   이번 여름은 _____

3. 주말에 춤을 춰요.
   이번 주말에 _____

4. 이번 주말에 뭐 할 거예요? (Make your own answer.)
   _____

나 Change the following verbs ending with the vowel "ㅣ" into the V어요 form.

1. 내리다 _____

2. 다니다 _____

3. 기다리다 _____

4. 마시다 _____

다 Answer the following questions.

1. 한국말 공부하기가 어때요? 쉬워요?

_____

2. 일하기가 어때요? 힘들어요?

_____

3. 서울에서 운전하기가 어때요? 괜찮아요?

_____

라 Practice the following situation with a friend.

What kind of weather do you like? Have a discussion with a friend about the kinds of weather that you like, places you like to travel to in order to experience that weather, and how you like to get there.

CHAPTER 15

It doesn't help

도움이 안 돼요

Maybe it was that plane flight, or maybe it was the crowded 극장 (movie theater), but somewhere along the way John must have come into contact with someone who was sick. He is not feeling so well. It seems that he has caught a 감기 (cold). 유식, like any good friend, shows his concern by asking "어디 아파요?" (What's wrong? / Where does it hurt?). And the next question that any good Korean friend would ask is of course "약을 먹었어요?" (Did you take medicine?). Finally 유식 recommends heading to the hospital. John agrees that it seems as though that is the only option.

Dialog

존	감기에 걸린 것 같아요.
유식	그래요? 어디 아파요?
존	콧물이 나오고 머리가 아파요.
유식	약 먹었어요?
존	네, 그렇지만 도움이 안 돼요.
유식	이상하네요. 그러면 병원에 가야 되죠.
존	그렇게 해야 될 것 같아요.

John Cold caught seems like.
Yoo-shik Really? Where hurt?
John Snot come out and head hurt.
Yoo-shik Medicine ate?
John Yes. But help not become.
Yoo-shik Strange wow. Then hospital go have to.
John Like that have to do it seems.

John	I think I've caught a cold.
Yoo-shik	Really? What's wrong?
John	I've got a runny nose and a headache.
Yoo-shik	Did you take any medicine?
John	Yes. But it didn't help.
Yoo-shik	That's strange. Then you'd better go see a doctor.
John	It seems as though I'll have to do that.

Key Expressions

감기에 걸렸어요. I caught a cold.

머리가 아파요. I have a headache.

콧물이 나와요. I have a runny nose.

약을 먹어요. Take medicine.

도움이 안 돼요. It doesn't (didn't) help.

이상하네요. That's strange.

그렇게 해야 될 것 같아요. It seems I'll have to do that.

감기 a cold

걸리다 to catch

V은/는/을 것 같다 It seems as though, I think

아프다 to hurt

콧물 snot

머리 head

약 medicine

도움 help (noun form of 돕다—to help)

되다 to be, to become

병원 hospital

이상하다 to be strange

Bonus Vocabulary

치료 Treatment, cure

병원 hospital, clinic   약국 pharmacy
증상 symptom   진찰 examination
주사 an injection

어디 아파요? Where does it hurt?

감기에 걸리다 to catch a cold   소화가 안 되다 to have indigestion
속이 쓰리다 to have heartburn   머리가 아프다 to have a headache
배가 아프다 to have a stomachache
허리가 아프다 to have a lower-back ache
쑤시다 to throb   붓다 to swell

의사 Doctors

내과 의사 doctor of internal medicine
외과 의사 surgeon
성형외과 의사 plastic surgeon
이비인후과 의사 ear/nose/throat doctor
산부인과 의사 obstetrician/gynecologist (ObGyn)
소아과 의사 pediatrician

Getting It

》Sentence Ending

N인 것 같다, A(으)ㄴ 것 같다, V(으)ㄴ/는/(으)ㄹ 것 같다
_It seems as though ~, I think ~

This is a very common ending in Korean, and it's common not just because it is useful, but also because of Korean culture (more on this later). Koreans often use this ending to politely give their opinions even if it is something they are obviously sure of. Remember how I said using the correct tense was very important? Well, it's very important here too. As you have seen, past gets (으)ㄴ, present gets 는, and future V gets (으)ㄹ. Use **N인 것 같다, A(으)ㄴ 것 같다, V(으)ㄴ/는/(으)ㄹ 것 같다** is for conjecture and/or giving opinions politely.

You've been working at Korean for a while now, and it seems like it is very difficult. How do you tell people you find it extremely challenging?

아주 어려운 것 같아요.

And since it is so difficult, it seems like you will have to study a lot ~

공부 많이 해야 될 것 같아요.

Your friend, who hears this, observes that you seem to be studying very hard:

공부 열심히 하는 것 같아요.

He's right. You're starting to make some serious progress.

》Korean Key

1. This one is really easy to remember. You saw in the dialog that Yoo-shik asked if John had taken medicine. How did he do it? He said, "약을 먹었어요?" **Use the verb for "to eat" (먹다) when referring to taking medicine.**

(In English, when someone says something that sounds crazy, you may ask, "Are you on drugs?" In Korean you can ask, "약 먹었어요?" Of course, only with good friends!)

2 We're back again with this verb with seemingly infinite meanings, 되다. First of all, remember that it is 되+어요 that results in 돼요. The pronunciation ends up the same, but you need to know how to spell it correctly. In today's dialog, John says, "도움이 안 돼요."—It's not helpful. The main thing to understand is that 되다 is used for a wide variety of changes. Hence it could refer to becoming something, making something, giving something, etc., etc. Here are some more examples (you will understand soon.)

이해가 될 거예요.

It will all turn out well, trust me.

다 잘 될 거예요.

In 3 months you'll be great at Korean.

3개월 되면 잘 할 거예요.

This is a very common format. (Time period)+되면=in (time period)

〉〉 Pronunciation

In today's dialog you heard 그렇지만 and 그렇게. Did you notice the pronunciation of each of those was a little bit different than you might have originally guessed? That ㅎ is kind of like just sending air out of your mouth when it is pronounced, right? That's what it does when it hits another consonant that can be aspirated; it forces air out of your mouth. **Any consonant that can be aspirated is aspirated when it comes after a** ㅎ 받침. Which consonants can be aspirated? For most, you just add a line:

ㄱ → ㅋ
ㄷ → ㅌ
ㅂ → ㅍ
ㅈ → ㅊ

So here are some words you already know and their pronunciation:

좋다 [조타]

그렇지만 [그러치만]

그렇게 [그러케]

Understanding the Korean World

    The first thing you will hear from a Korean person when you get sick is, "약 먹었어요?" There are two reasons for this. The first is that this is another one of the many ways that Koreans show they care for their friends. All winter long one of the most common things to say before you leave someone is "감기 조심하세요!" (Be careful of colds!). You can see how showing concern for your friends is a perennial task in Korean society. These small but essential signs of affection are part of the art of being a good friend and member of '우리'.

    The second reason is that taking medicine for even a small cold is much more common than in most places. I think part of the reason is that only a few years ago pharmacists were not far off from doctors, since prescriptions were not necessary to get medicine. Although the law changed in 1999, and you need a prescription to get most medicines now, as soon as you get sick you'll still be given the advice to take medicine ASAP. Sometimes it's just better to tell a little white lie like, "네, 먹었어요." than to try to resist the pressure to take it.

Exercises

가 Make some inferences about what happened using V(으)ㄴ 것 같아요.

1. 존이 술을 마셨어요?

   _____

2. 진호가 숙제를 했어요?

   _____

3. 그 학생이 책을 읽었어요?

   _____

나 You're on the phone with three different people. Make some inferences from the background noise about what the person is doing using V는 것 같아요.

1. 텔레비전 보고 있어요?

2. 버스를 타고 있어요?

3. 지금 뭐 먹고 있어요?

다 Make some inferences about the following.

1. 존이 늦을까요?

2. 그 남자가 운동을 잘 할까요?

3. 비가 올까요?

라 Practice the following situation with a friend.

Tell your partner about the worst sickness you ever got. What were your symptoms? How long were you sick? What did you do to recover? Make sure you use past tense.

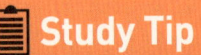

Study Tip

Watch Out for Transference Errors!

What do I mean by transference errors? It's when you try to make Korean into English. When I was starting to learn Korean, I still remember walking around and saying to my friends, "기다릴 수 없어요!" when I was excited about an upcoming event. Every time I did, they would look at me with a blank stare: that stare you get when they are trying to put together what the heck you are trying to say. You see, in Korean you don't say, "I can't wait!" when you are excited about an upcoming event. It just doesn't make sense. You say, "기대가 돼요!" That means, "to expect" something, and if you spend any time with Koreans learning English you will hear them say, "I'm expecting it" when they should be saying, "I'm looking forward to it." These are transference errors.

How can you avoid them? That's what I'm here for. Here are some of the most common transference errors that native English speakers make when starting out:

1) You can't "love" a food. In Korea, you only love people, and sometimes maybe a country. DO NOT say, "김치를 사랑해요." It's "김치를 정말 좋아해요."

2) You don't ask for permission by saying, "Can I...?" Of course it is physically possible; you're just asking permission. It's just like when you watch an old movie and the child says to her/his parent, "Can I have one?" Then the parent scolds the child, "Not, 'Can I?'—'May I?'" It's the same idea. So don't say, "할 수 있어요?" when asking permission, say, "해도 돼요?"

3) Do not raise your intonation when saying, "네." In English this can provide emphasis to your response, but in Korean it means, "Excuse me, I couldn't hear you." I can't tell you how many times I had people repeat themselves when I already understood what they said. It drove me nuts for years until I finally understood that the mistake was mine!

CHAPTER 16
How long does it take?
얼마나 걸려요?

Getting sick was the last straw for John. 유식 told him that there is a warmer place in Korea: 제주도! Often called "The Korean Hawaii", 제주도 is warmer in the winter and cooler in the summer than the mainland. Flight tickets aren't too expensive either, and that has brought John to the 여행사 (travel agent) today. He plans on going to 제주도 next month, so he is making a 예약 (reservation). He walks in and tells the agent that he wants to make a reservation for departing on 삼월 십칠일. She of course wants to know when he plans to 돌아오다 (come back, return). He's going to return 삼월 이십일일에. She takes a moment to input his dates into the computer and his reservation is made. Having never gone to 제주도 before, John is of course wondering how long the flight will take. 한 시간 정도—About an hour.

직원	어서 오세요. 어떻게 오셨어요?
존	3월 17일에 제주도에 가려고 해요.
직원	며칠에 돌아오실 거예요?
존	3월 21일에 돌아오려고 해요.
직원	네, 잠시만요. 3월 17일에 출발해서 21일 돌아오는 것으로 예약이 됐어요, 손님.
존	서울에서 제주도까지 얼마나 걸려요?
직원	한 시간 정도 걸려요.

Travel Agent Hurry come in. How come did?
John March 17th Chejudo go plan to.
Travel Agent What day back come plan to?
John March 21st back come plan to.
Travel Agent Yes, moment only. March 17th depart 21st back come reservation made, customer.
John Seoul from Chejudo to time how much take?
Travel Agent One hour about take.

Travel agent	Welcome. What can I do for you?
John	I plan on going to Chejudo on March 17th.
Travel agent	What day would you like to return?
John	I plan on coming back on the 21st.
Travel agent	Okay, just a minute. Your reservation departing on the 17th and returning on the 21st is all set, sir.
John	How long is the flight from Seoul to Chejudo?
Travel agent	It takes about 1 hour.

Key Expressions

어서 오세요. Come in. (Welcome.)

어떻게 오셨어요? How can I help you?

가려고 해요. I plan on going.

며칠에 가려고 해요? What day do you plan on going?

21일에 돌아오려고 해요. I plan on returning on the 21st.

P₁에서 P₂까지 얼마나 걸려요? How long does it take to get from P₁ to P₂?*

두 시간 반 걸려요. It takes two and a half hours.

어서	quickly	돕다	to help
일	day	며칠	what day
돌아오다	to come back	V(으)려고 하다	to plan to V
출발하다	to depart	예약	reservation
P에서	from P*	N까지	to N
시간	time	얼마나	how much
걸리다	to take	정도	about

★ P=place

➕ Bonus Vocabulary

여행 Travel

여행하다 to travel
예약 a reservation
예약을 취소하다 to cancel a reservation
왕복 round trip

구경하다 to sightsee
예약하다 to make a reservation

편도 one-way

숙박 Lodging

호텔 hotel
온돌방 traditional Korean room (floor mats, no bed)
침대 bed

여관, 모텔 motel

침대 방 room with a bed

수식어 Modifiers

N 정도, N쯤 about N

거의 almost

집 The house

부엌 kitchen
안방 master bedroom
거실 family/living room

침실 bedroom
옷장 closet

Getting It

〉〉 Sentence Ending

V(으)려고 하다   _to plan to V

One of the more easy endings to understand and use, "V(으)려고 하다" means that one plans to V.

Obviously if you bought this book, this sentence refers to you:

한국말을 배우려고 해요.

Do you ever plan on going to Korea?

당연히 가려고 해요.

Good for you. Now finally, 저녁에 뭘 먹으려고 해요?

갈비나 불고기 먹으려고 해요.

That's what foreigners always eat. I really suggest some 닭갈비. Try some other Korean food too. It's addictive.

〉〉 Auxiliary

(P에서/T부터) N까지   _(from N) to N*

Now there are two different beginnings for this one, but they are the same word in English—from. You learned that "에서" is used for the location of actions and origins. Here it is again, used as "from" but I have to teach you another auxiliary as well because "T부터 T까지" is "from N to N" used when discussing a time period, while "P에서 P까지 is "from N to N" when used for a change in locations and other nouns.

★ P=place, T=time

Do you know how long the flight from Seoul to LA is?

서울에서 LA까지 11시간 정도 걸려요.

So if you get on the plane at 8 in the morning Seoul time, until what time will you be stuck on the plane?

오전 8시부터 오후 7시까지 타야 돼요.

Will that be fun?

아니요, 처음부터 끝까지 힘들 거예요.

This is a very common expression in Korean. From the beginning to the end, from start to finish ~

처음부터 끝까지

》Conjunction

V_1여/아/어서 V_2 _V_1 and then V_2

John is going to take off and then come back again. The conjunction "V여/아/어서" shows that an action takes place that is necessary before another follows. It shows the order that things occur in.

First you have to find the restaurant before you can eat there.

식당을 찾아서 뭘 좀 먹어요.

And you need to go to the office before you can do your work.

회사에 가서 일해요.

Finally you should know that learning Korean will help you meet some great friends.

한국말 배워서 한국친구 만나요.

And remember, "Nice to meet you."?

만나서 반갑습니다.

〉〉 Korean Key

There are a couple of questions that may leave you taken aback if you don't know better. The first you saw in our dialog. "어떻게 오셨어요?" literally translated means, "How did you come here?" If you answer you came by bus or by taxi, you'll get a puzzled or bemused look from your questioner. That's because 90% of the time the actual thing they want to know is WHY you came, not your means of transportation. It would be really rude to say, "Why did you come here?" because it would almost imply that they would rather you hadn't come.

The other one you will get when you call someone on the phone. If you make a call to an office, don't be surprised when the secretary answering says, "어디세요?" No, they don't want to know where you are calling from. They want to know who you are. Again, simply asking, "누구세요?" to someone calling would be too direct. Indirect is a little more polite.

Understanding the Korean World

Traveling in Korea is the best way to experience this country. Seoul is a big metropolis, which is nice, but it's not the best of what Korea has to offer. As is the case with most major cities in the world, the people tend to get friendlier the farther you get from Seoul. Korea has over 3,000 islands as well as beautiful beaches, mountains and valleys. Trains, buses and ferries can get you to places so remote that you will wonder how the government can afford to operate the routes. Motels and 민박 (home stays) are cheap and numerous. It also happens to be one of the most crime-free countries in the world. It truly is the undiscovered backpacker's paradise (but the coffee gets worse the farther you get from Seoul, so make the necessary preparations).

When picking a motel, consider an 온돌방, especially if you are traveling with someone you'd rather not share a bed with. The floor mats they give are usually thick and comfortable, and the heating system is in the floor, so it's warm and toasty in the winter. It's better for your back to sleep on the floor anyway. If you think you can't take it, however, you can request a 침대방.

Exercises

가 Make a sentence using the following words and V(으)려고 해요.

1. 여름, 존, 여행하다

2. 오늘 6시, 친구, 만나다

3. 혜숙 씨, 이따가, 공부하다

4. 선생님, 책, 읽다

나 Add the correct auxiliary.

1. 9시___ 12시___ 공부하려고 해요.

2. 서울역___ 부산역___ 5시간 걸려요.

3. 학교___ 집___ 버스를 타요.

4. 그 영화는 처음___ 끝___ 재미없었어요.

다 Practice the following situation with a friend.

Why are you studying Korean? Do you have any special plans? Talk about what you plan on doing once you become fluent in Korean.

CHAPTER 17 | I'm thirty
만으로 서른 살이에요

John's had about a month in Seoul now, and now he gets to head to 제주도. He's really excited about his trip, and when he gets on the plane he gets even more excited. That's because a beautiful young lady is in the seat next to him.

Three important points before you hear the introductions. First of all, knowing someone's age is very important in Korea as age determines many aspects of a relationship immediately, including how you will speak to each other. Hence, people you just meet will often ask your age. Next you need to know that people will often refer to their older friend as "older brother" or "older sister," again contributing to that feeling of closeness that is so important in Korean relationships. Finally, there are two kinds of age in Korea; Korean age and the age the rest of the world uses. By Korean age you're always a year or two older than your birth date. To say, "in Korean age" you say "한국 나이로", and to say by birth age you say, "만으로".

존	안녕하세요. 저는 존이라고 해요. 성함이 어떻게 되세요?
지혜	저는 지혜라고 해요.
존	만나서 반갑습니다. 실례지만, 지혜 씨는 나이가 어떻게 되세요?
지혜	저는 77년생이에요. 한국 나이로 스물아홉 살이에요.
존	그럼, 전 지혜 씨의 오빠가 되네요. 75년생이니까요. 만으로 서른 살이에요.

John Hello. I John am called. Name how made up?
Ji-hae I Ji-hae am called.
John Nice to meet you. Rude act but Ji-hae age how constituted?
Ji-hae I 77 year born am. Korea age by 29 years am.
John Then I Ji-hae's older brother become wow! 75 year born because. Normal age by 30 years am.

John	Hello. My name is John. What's your name?
Ji-hae	I'm Ji-hae.
John	Nice to meet you. Excuse me, but how old are you?
Ji-hae	I was born in 77. In Korean age I am 29.
John	That would make me older, since I was born in 75. I'm 30 in normal age.

Key Expressions

저는 ~(이)라고 해요. My name is ~. (I am called ~.)

성함이 어떻게 되세요? What is your name? (formal)

나이가 어떻게 되세요? How old are you? (formal)

~년생이에요. I was born in ~.

한국 나이로 ~살이에요. By Korean age (one) is ~ years old.

만으로 ~살이에요. By normal age (one) is ~ years old.

~(이)라고 하다 to be called ~

되다 to be made up or constituted as

년생 year born (noun)

오빠 older brother (to a female)

살 counter for years of age

성함 name (honorific form)

나이 age

한국 나이 Korean age

만 birth age

 Bonus Vocabulary

몇 살이에요? How old are you?

살 counter for years of age (pure Korean numbers)
세 counter for years of age (Sino-Korean numbers)

Pure Korean numbers

열 10   스물 20   서른 30
마흔 40   쉰 50   예순 60
일흔 70   여든 80   아흔 90
백 100 (always change to Sino-Korean numbers after 100)

가구 Furniture

의자 chair   소파 sofa   책상 desk
책장 bookshelf   서랍장 dresser   식탁 kitchen table
테이블, 탁자 table

Getting It

>> **Sentence Ending**

N(이)라고 하다 _to be called N

Does this look familiar to you? If you memorized the expressions in the first study tip, then it should. There I taught you how to ask what something is called in Korean. Today you're learning a new, formal way to introduce yourself using the same sentence ending. "N(이)라고 하다" **tells how to refer to someone or something.**

What's the expression for asking what something is called in Korean?

한국말로 뭐라고 해요?

And how would someone respond if they were teaching you what a bed is called in Korean?

이것은 침대라고 해요.

Now let's say you're at the airport, and you forgot the word for airplane. Ask away:

저것은 뭐라고 해요?

And of course they will come back with:

비행기라고 해요.

John is in a 비행기, right now and that's why he needs the next phrase to talk to the person next to him.

>> **Sentence**

N이/가 어떻게 되세요? _What is N? Tell me about N.

This isn't just an ending, it's a full sentence that is used so often that I'm dedicating a section to it. This is a use of the verb "되다" that does not deal with change of any kind. It asks about circumstances, situations and the make-up of things. "N이/가 어떻게 되세요?" **can be used to politely inquire about any place or thing.** You may wonder why John and Yoo-shik didn't use it, and that would be because they were introduced by someone else, so there was already a relationship there. This is used more often with people who don't know each other at all, or to people in a much senior position.

It is also usually used with the most formal nouns too. Remember how there were different verbs for formal expressions? Well, guess what? You get to learn double words for certain nouns too! I told you this stuff was an art.

The formal word for name is 성함:

성함이 어떻게 되세요?

You heard the normal word for age above (나이) but there is also a formal word that needs to be used with senior people:

연세가 어떻게 되세요?

If you're familiar with the most famous university in Korea then it shouldn't be hard to remember this word.

You could also ask about someone's family with this expression:

가족은 어떻게 되세요?

>> **Auxiliary**

N(으)로 _by N, according to N

We already saw this when we were giving directions, and you've seen it in some phrases as well. Now it takes a new meaning in today's dialog. **N(으)로 is used for "by N" or "according to N".** I taught you this already, didn't I? In teaching you to ask how to say something in Korean, we said:

이거 한국말로 뭐예요?

I can hear you now. "It's missing the 받침 enabler even though there is a 받침" you're shouting, right? This is an irregular. The rest of the time anything with a 받침 gets the 받침 enabler vowel, but in this case since the 받침 is a ㄹ, it actually becomes more difficult to pronounce if the vowel is there. Don't believe me? You try saying, "한국말으로." Difficult, isn't it?

But I digress—back to the point. We saw today that we talked about measuring age in different ways using 한국나이로 and 만으로. That's another instance. You could also tell someone the method of transportation you will use for your trip with this as well.

기차로 갈 거예요.

Enjoy the ride. Korean trains are the best.

Understanding the Korean World

Is the culture shock kicking in yet? It's unimaginable in most societies; the second question after meeting someone is "How old are you?" There's more to come. Part of becoming friends in Korea is getting to know someone with what may seem like very intimate and personal questions. Sometimes questions or comments will seem to the untrained ear to be insults.

Another shocker is when a Koreans point out that someone should lose or gain weight, or mentions a recent weight loss or gain. They don't say this to be offensive, but just the opposite. It is to show that they are worried about the person they are talking to. I once worked on a show with a writer and I saw her every two weeks for three years. We became great friends and I still consider her one of my best friends in Korea. I didn't need to bother with scales back when I was working with her. She kept me updated on my gain or loss just fine. 연진, I hope you're doing well. And you should know that I lost 3 kgs.

Exercises

가 Answer the following questions.

1. 사람들이 일하는 곳을 뭐라고 해요?

| | | | | | | |

2. 사람들이 사는 곳을 뭐라고 해요?

| | | | | | | |

3. 책이 많고 사람들이 공부하는 곳을 뭐라고 해요?

| | | | | | | | |

나 Politely ask someone you just met about the following.

1. Their name:

   _____

2. Their family:

   _____

3. Their age:

   _____

다 Practice the following situation with a friend.

You just sat down next to a rather attractive person on the train and you're in for a long ride together. Make some conversation.

CHAPTER 18
Do you have any brothers or sisters?
형제가 어떻게 되세요?

It's a short flight to 제주도, and it's made even shorter by the fact that John and 지혜 are having a great conversation. Now the topic is family: an important topic in any country. First John asks 지혜 if she lives on 제주도. She responds that she does and adds that she lives with her 부모님 (parents), although she wishes she lived alone. John asks about her 형제 (siblings) and he finds out that she is the 막내 (youngest). John, it turns out, is the youngest as well and wishes he had a younger sibling.

You're going to hear 지혜 talk about her older brothers and sisters and you'll hear John talk about his older brothers and sisters, but you won't hear either of them use the same words. That's because the words are different based on whether you are a man or a woman. For a woman the older sister is 언니 and her older brother is 오빠. For a man his older sister is 누나 and his older brother is 형.

Dialog

존	지혜 씨는 제주도에서 사세요?
지혜	네, 부모님하고 같이 살아요. 혼자 살았으면 좋겠어요.
존	형제는 어떻게 되세요?
지혜	오빠 하나, 언니 둘이 있어요.
존	막내네요.
지혜	네. 존 씨는요?
존	저도 막내예요. 누나 하나, 형 하나 있어요. 동생이 있었으면 좋겠어요.

John Ji-hea Ms. Chejudo at live?
Ji-hae Yes. Parents with together live. Alone lived if good would.
John Siblings how composed?
Ji-hae Older brother one, older sister two have.
John Youngest wow.
Ji-hae Yes. John what about?
John Me too youngest. Older sister, older brother have. Younger sibling had if good would be.

John	Do you live on Cheju island, Ji-hae?
Ji-hae	Yes, I live with my parents. I wish I lived alone.
John	Do you have any brothers and sisters?
Ji-hae	One older brother and two older sisters.
John	So you're the youngest.
Ji-hae	Right. How about you?
John	I'm the youngest too. I have an older sister and an older brother. I wish I had a younger brother or sister.

Key Expressions

N에(서) 사세요? Do you live at (in) N?

어디 사세요? Where do you live?

V였/았/었으면 좋겠어요. I wish V., I would like to V.

N에 살아요. I live at (in, on) N.

P하고 같이 살아요. I live with P.*

N이/가 있었으면 좋겠어요. I wish I had a N., It would be nice if I had an N.

살다 to live
부모(님) parents
오빠 older brother (to a female)
막내 the youngest
아주 very
형 older brother (to a male)

혼자 alone
형제 siblings
언니 older sister (to a female)
가족 family
누나 older sister (to a male)
동생 younger sibling (genderless term)

* P=person

Bonus Vocabulary

아이들 Children

형제 siblings   자매 sisters
장남 first born son   장녀 first born daughter
막내 youngest   아들 son   딸 daughter
외동아들 only child (son)   외동딸 only child (daughter)
남동생 younger brother   여동생 younger daughter
오빠 older brother (to a female)   언니 older sister (to a female)
형 older brother (to a male)   누나 older sister (to a male)

어른들 Adults

할아버지 grandfather   할머니 grandmother
아버지 father   아빠 dad
어머니 mother   엄마 mom
삼촌 uncle (on your father's side)   외삼촌 uncle (on your mother's side)
고모 aunt (on your father's side)   이모 aunt (on your mother's side)

수식어 Modifiers

아주 very (colloquial)   매우 very (more formal, written)
정말, 진짜 really   너무 too   조금 a little

"르" 불규칙 동사 Irregular "르" verbs

살다 to live   벌다 to earn   놀다 to play

Getting It

》Irregular verb

Irregular "ㄹ" verb

The advantage of this one is that the "ㄹ" just drops off. The disadvantage is that it's tough to know when to keep it, and when to drop it. **For irregular "ㄹ" verbs, the "ㄹ" drops when it come before ㄴ, ㅂ, and ㅅ**. Here is some practice for you:

No change before vowels:

어디 살아요?

But when you put it before ㄴ, like V는데, then there goes that ㄹ:

신촌에 사는데, 너무 시끄러워요.

Same when it comes before a ㅅ, like when you add the polite ending V(으)세요:

혼자 사세요?

》Auxiliary

P하고 같이 V _to do V with P★

You know 하고 means "and," and you know that 같이 means "together." Now you saw that you can use both of them at the same time. It may seem a little redundant, but Korean is not nearly as concerned about following the rules as English is. So let me give you some examples of how these two are used in combination.

★ P=person

Did you meet your sister alone?

아니요, 친구하고 같이 만났어요.

Who are you going to see the movie with?

지혜하고 같이 볼 거예요.

What are you going to do on the weekend?

부모님하고 같이 여행할 거예요.

You're going to travel with your parents? That'll be nice.

⟩⟩ Sentence Ending

V였/았/었으면 좋겠어요. _I wish V. / I would like to V.

We're combining a lot of things you already know to come up with this sentence ending. It starts out with the past tense auxiliary, then the conjunction meaning "if" and then it ends with what we have learned—the future tense auxiliary. While we have a different word for this expression (we use "would" instead of "will"), in Korean they use the same word for both. **V 였/았/었으면 좋겠어요. means you would like it if V were true or real.**

Here's one I know is true for you:

한국말 잘 했으면 좋겠어요.

And here's one that true for everyone:

돈이 많았으면 좋겠어요.

And here's one that's true for me:

결혼했으면 좋겠어요.

Someday I'll get married. But I wish that someday were yesterday.

〉〉 Pronunciation

ㄱ 받침 before ㄴ/ㄹ/ㅁ → ㅇ 받침

I'm sure you heard it—the ㄱ at the end of the first syllable in 막내. Why doesn't that sound like a "g," you're wondering? It's another rule that when the 'ㄱ' 받침 comes before a syllable starting with ㄴ/ㄹ or ㅁ, then it is pronounced as a 'ㅇ'. There's a street in northern Seoul that is the location of Korea's oldest university and used to be home to Seoul National University, so they call it university street:

대학로 [대항노]

And that is an example of a Sino-Korean word. You can take 학 meaning school and place that before 년 meaning year and you get the word for someone's grade level.

학년 [항년]

And you've heard this enough that you probably caught it on your own.

한국말 [한궁말]

Understanding the Korean World

The first born son is gold in Korea. Until only a generation ago, when daughters married into another family, it was for real. The woman had little to no contact with her original family. It was the oldest son's job to take care of his parents into old age, so a couple without a son could count on a pitiful existence in later life. This sense of responsibility still exists, and many families keep trying to have children until they get a son. I can't tell you how many families I've met with two, three, four or more daughters and the youngest is a son. I met one man with 8 older sisters! This extreme preference for sons combined with modern medicine has had some undesired results. Korea has one of the highest differences in gender birth rates in the world. This extreme desire for a son apparently peaked in 1995, when the birth rate hit 113 boys for every 100 girls. It is obviously changing quickly now. I meet more and more parents and even college students these days who want nothing but to have a daughter.

Exercises

가 Conjugate the using the irregular "ㄹ" verbs given.

1. 돈은 많이 ____는데 시간이 없어요. (벌다)

2. 어디 ____세요? (살다)

3. 신촌에서 ____니까 매일 ____아요. (살다, 놀다)

4. 매일 ____니까 돈을 못 ____어요. (놀다, 벌다)

나 Rewrite the sentence as a wish.

1. 돈이 있어요.

2. 예뻐요.

3. 한국말을 잘 할 수 있어요.

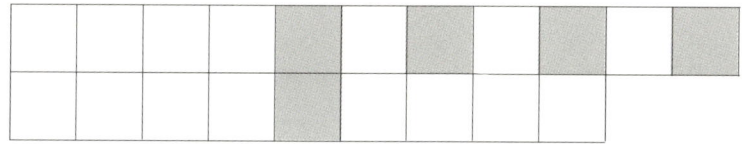

4. 노래를 잘 해요.

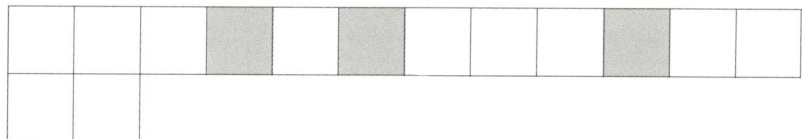

라 Practice the following situation with a friend.

No family is perfect. Tell your partner about your family, and some ways in which you wish it were just a bit different.

CHAPTER 19
It doesn't matter
상관없어요

John and 지혜 continue to get to know each other. As we all know, one of the best ways to ingratiate yourself to people is to give them a compliment. John tells 지혜 that she's 예뻐요 (pretty) and 지혜 says that John is 잘생겼어요 (handsome) himself. Then they compliment something that the other is wearing. 지혜 likes John's sunglasses and John appreciates 지혜's skirt. John then makes an invitation to 산책하다 (go for a walk) tomorrow. 지혜 likes the idea, but she apparently has plans in the morning. She asks if it's okay to go in the 오후 (afternoon). John doesn't care. He's perfectly happy with the afternoon too.

Dialog

존	지혜 씨, 정말 예뻐요.
지혜	뭘요. 존 씨도 잘생겼어요. 그리고 그 선글라스도 진짜 마음에 들어요.
존	고마워요. 그 치마도 지혜 씨한테 잘 어울리는데요.
지혜	별말씀을요.
존	지혜 씨, 내일 바닷가에 가서 산책할래요?
지혜	진짜요? 좋죠. 그런데 오후에 가도 돼요?
존	상관없어요. 오후도 좋아요.

John Ji-hae Ms. very pretty.
Ji-hae What. John mister too well made up. Those sunglasses too really heart appeals to.
John Thanks. That skirt Ji-hae Ms. to well looks good on.
Ji-hae Special speech.
John Ji-hae Ms. Tomorrow beach go and walk want to?
Ji-hae Really? Good. But afternoon in go okay?
John Matter doesn't have. Afternoon too good.

John	You're very pretty, Ji-hae.
Ji-hae	Not at all. You're very handsome. I really like those sunglasses too.
John	Thanks. That skirt really looks good on you.
Ji-hae	Oh, you're flattering me.
John	Would you like to go to the beach and go for a walk tomorrow?
Ji-hae	Really? Sounds great. But can we go in the afternoon?
John	It doesn't matter. The afternoon is fine.

Key Expressions

잘생겼어요. (One) is handsome.

마음에 들어요. I like it.

잘 어울려요. It looks good on (someone).

별말씀을요. Oh, you're just flattering me.

할래요? Would you like to do it?

산책할래요? Would you like to go for a walk?

해도 돼요? May I do it?

가도 돼요? May I go?

상관없어요. It doesn't matter. (I don't care.)

아주 very
잘생겼다 to be handsome
진짜 really
치마 skirt
어울리다 to match well, to look good on one
산책하다 to go for a walk
오후 afternoon
상관 concern

예쁘다 pretty
선글라스 sunglasses
마음 heart, mind
N한테 to N

V(으)ㄹ래요? Want to V?
V여/아/어도 돼요? May I V?

Bonus Vocabulary

외모 Appearance

예쁘다 to be pretty
못생겼다 to be ugly
아름답다 to be beautiful

잘생겼다 to be handsome
귀엽다 to be cute
멋있다 to be cool (looking)

옷 Clothing

티셔츠 T-shirt
스웨터 sweater
바지 pants
반바지 short
미니스커트 miniskirt
선글라스 sunglasses
운동화 gym shoes, sneakers

와이셔츠 dress shirt
재킷 jacket
치마 skirt
청바지 (blue) jeans
모자 hat
구두 dress shoes

Wearing stuff

입다 to put on, to wear (clothes)
신다 to put on, to wear (shoes or socks)
차다 to put on, to wear (a watch)
쓰다 to put on, to wear (a hat or glasses)
벗다 to take off (all of the above)

Getting It

〉〉 Sentence Ending

1 V(으)ㄹ래요? _Do you want to V?

We've already learned some more formal expressions for this kind of thing. Do you remember "V(으)시겠어요"? You can consider that kind of saying, "Would you like to V?" This one is slightly more casual, and therefore used more between acquaintances, and the former is for complete strangers. "V(으)ㄹ래요?" **is used for inviting someone to do something.**

Let's say you and a friend are talking about going somewhere, and another friend hears you. You could invite her/him along:

갈래요? (or for a much older friend, 가실래요?)

How about asking someone if they would like to eat something?

먹을래요? (If they are older it would be "드실래요?")

And now that you've eaten with them, let's be more productive. Let's invite them to study Korean together:

한국말을 같이 공부할래요?

Studying with a partner is one of the best ways to study.

This ending can also be used to say what you will do, or tell plans for the future. There are a lot of ways to say this, aren't there? When you use this one it is a little stronger. It kind of implies that you will do it regardless of whether anyone objects, so try to stick to using it with close friends.

Let's say a friend asks you what you want to do, and you're really hungry ~

난 밥 먹을래요.

Another friend may respond ~

난 술 마실래요.

Then the peacemaker will say ~

밥 먹고 술 마실까요?

That should satisfy both of you.

2 V여/아/어도 돼요?   _May I (one) V?

We learned how to ask if someone "can" do something, but that speaks strictly of possibility, not permission. "V여/아/어도 돼요" **is used for asking and giving permission.**

Let's say this time that you are walking around the department store, and someone is handing out free samples. You want to ask permission before taking one, right?

먹어도 돼요?

그럼요! (Sure!)

Now you're looking at some shoes that you really like, and you want to try them on. Ask permission for that one:

신어도 돼요?

One of the most difficult things about Korean—they have different verbs for "to wear" depending on what you are wearing. It is complicated, but just remember these two first—입다 for pants, jackets, shirts, etc., and 신다 for shoes and socks.

You're still at the department store, but this time you are looking at a display model, and you want to ask if you can buy it:

사도 돼요?

〉〉 **Auxiliary**

P한테 _to P, on P*

That skirt looks good on 지혜. Did you catch that when you talk about something looking good on someone you have to say the person's name and attach 한테? **P한테 means something is 'to', 'on' or otherwise related to a person.**

You can go to a person:

친구한테 가요.

Or something can be difficult to you especially:

저한테는 어려워요.

This last one implies that it's more difficult to you than most because of that contrastive marker 은/는 attached to the end. So you can't use that sentence for Korean. Languages are difficult for most everyone!

★ P=person

Understanding the Korean World

Dating customs in Korea are VERY different from most countries that I know of. Traditionally marriages were arranged. "선" is the term for a meeting arranged by two sets of parents between their children. Until only a generation ago a "선" was a very official occasion in which both sets of parents participated. The potential bride and her parents would sit across the table from the groom and his parents and they would pretty much grill each other for a while. This formal meeting has all but disappeared and now just the man and woman meet for a modern "선", but it's still arranged.

Some more casual meeting methods would include 미팅 and 소개팅. At a 미팅 a girl and guy who are friends will each get two or three of their friends and they will start off with some discussions and then play games to see who ends up with each other. 소개팅 is pretty much the equivalent of a blind date. Notice Koreans don't often meet people without an introduction; it is rather uncommon for people to date someone they haven't been introduced to by a third party in some fashion.

Exercises

가 Invite someone to try the following.

1. 같이 밥(을) 먹다.

   | | | | | | | | | ?

2. 농구하다.

   | | | | | | ?

3. 이 셔츠(를) 입다.

   | | | | | | | | | ?

나 Tell someone what you intend to do.

1. 학교에 가다.

   _____

2. 학교에서 축구하다.

   _____

3. 바닷가에서 수영하다.

   _____

다 Ask permission for the following.

1. 이 찌개(를) 먹다.

   _____

2. 그 치마(를) 입다.

   _____

3. 내일 학교에 안 나오다.

   _____

4. 와인(을) 좀 마시다.

   _____

라 Practice the following situation with a friend.

You meet someone who you know is very powerful and could make a good friend. Introduce yourself and make sure you throw a few compliments into the conversation, and maybe even an invitation to get together again.

CHAPTER 20

Come hang out with me!
놀러 오세요!

John has gotten over his cold now. Thanks in large part to 지혜 he had a nice few days in 제주도 as well. But it's time to head back to Seoul. John invites 지혜 to 놀러 오세요 (come and hang out). Due to her line of work it is very likely that she will be headed to Seoul next month. If she is going to see him, however, she of course needs his 전화번호 (phone number). She tells John, "연락할게요" (I'll give you a call). John doesn't have any 명함 (business cards) with him, so he sends his 전화번호 by 문자 (text message). Then they say their goodbyes. 다음에 봐요! (See you next time). John gets on the bus to head to the airport.

Dialog

지혜	그동안 재미있었어요.
존	저도요. 서울에 한번 놀러 오세요.
지혜	일 때문에 아마 또 갈 거예요. 전화번호 가르쳐 주면 연락할게요.
존	명함이 없으니까 문자로 연락처를 보낼게요.
지혜	좋아요. 서울에 가면 그때 명함을 주세요.
존	그래요. 나중에 서울에서 봐요!
지혜	네, 꼭 전화할게요. 다음에 봐요!

Ji-hae That during fun had.
John Me too. Seoul to one time play to come.
Ji-hae Work because of maybe again go going to. Telephone number teach give if, call will if it's okay.
John Business card don't have so text message by contact number send will if it's okay.
Ji-hae That's okay. Seoul to go if then business card give please.
John Sure. Later Seoul in see!
Ji-hae Yes, definitely call if it's okay. Next time see!

Ji-hae	I had a nice time.
John	Me too. Next time come and spend time with me in Seoul.
Ji-hae	I might be going there again because of work. If you give me your number I'll give you a call.
John	I don't have any business cards right now so I'll send you my number by text message.
Ji-hae	That's okay. When I get to Seoul give me one then.
John	Sure. See you later in Seoul!
Ji-hae	Okay, I'll call you for sure. See you next time!

Key Expressions

그동안 재미있었어요. I had a nice time. (for extended time periods)

놀러 오세요. Come and spend time with me., Come and hang out.

아마 갈 거예요. Maybe one will go.

전화번호 가르쳐 주세요. Give me your phone number please.

전화번호 가르쳐 주면 연락할게요. If you give me your number, I'll give you a call.

문자로 보낼게요. I'll send it by text message.

N이/가 없으니까 지금 드릴 수 없어요. Because I don't have N I can't give it to you right now.

그때 주세요. Give it to me then.

꼭 전화할게요. I'll call you for sure.

다음에 봐요! See you next time!

그동안 during that time (long time period only)
놀다 to play, to spend time, to hang out
아마 maybe
또 again
번호 number
연락하다 to contact, to get in touch
연락처 contact number, address
보내다 to send
명함 business card
꼭 definitely

(한) 번 (one) time
N 때문에 because of N
전화 phone
문자 text message
그때 then

Bonus Vocabulary

의사소통 관련 명사 Communication nouns

전화 telephone   휴대폰 mobile phone
팩스 fax   이메일 e-mail
문자 text message 음성 (메시지) voice (message)
인터넷 Internet   자동응답기 automatic answering machine

의사소통 관련 동사 Communication verbs

연락하다 to contact, to get in touch with
전화하다 to call   보내다 to send
받다 to receive   문자를 보내다 to send a text message
전화를 받다 to answer the phone

액세서리 Accessories

목걸이 necklace   반지 ring
팔찌 bracelet   귀걸이 earrings
시계 watch, clock 안경 glasses
목도리 scarf   장갑 gloves

Getting It

〉〉 Korean Key

In English we typically only speak of children playing together, but in Korean often the word play, 놀다, is used to speak of spending time together and hanging out together. Here are some common expressions that can use this term:

놀러 오세요. Come hang out.

바닷가에 놀러 갑시다. Let's go hang out at the beach.

신촌에 가서 놀아요. Let's go have some fun in Seoul.

저는 노래방에서 노는 것이 좋아요. I like hanging out at a singing room.

같이 놀래요? Do you want to hang out?

〉〉 Auxiliary

N 동안 _for N, during N

This one is relatively easy to use. N 동안 **means for a time period or during a time period.** As always, some examples:

How long did you drink last night?

4시간 동안 술을 마셨어요.

How long did you study Korean?

2시간 동안 한국어 공부했어요.

And I'm sure you want to understand how this "during" thing works. You saw it above, when they said, "그동안 좋았어요."—It was nice during that time (our time together). Now here's one more:

방학 동안 공부 안 했어요. I didn't study during vacation.

I hope that's not true in your case.

〉〉 Conjunction

N 때문에 _because of N

Since we learned to say "because" in a different way (V(으)니까) this may seem a little redundant to you. Notice that this is not using a verb, but a noun. "N 때문에" **says that the reason for a (typically negative) result is N**. It's not always very negative, but rarely is this ever used for something very positive.

I hear you didn't go to class yesterday. Why?

감기 때문에 못 갔어요.

I'm sorry to hear that. You look okay, but you look a little tired.

약 때문에 졸려요.

You took a medicine that makes you drowsy. You should just go home.

숙제 때문에 못 가요.

You can't go because of homework? I'm sure the teacher will understand if you don't finish this on time.

내일 시험이 있기 때문에 오늘 해야 돼요.

You have a test tomorrow? Hurry up and finish so you can go to sleep! (Notice that you can use verbs by making them into nouns using "V기".)

>> **Pronunciation**

ㄴ 받침 before a ㄹ → ㄹ 받침

Did you catch the pronunciation of 연락하다? It's [열락하다], isn't it? That's because whenever a 'ㄴ' 받침 comes before a syllable starting with ㄹ, then it is pronounced as a ㄹ. That makes a nice long double 'l' sound, as you know. Here's a few more examples:

If you ride the subway down south on the #2 line you're likely to pass by a station called

선릉 [설릉]

There's also an old kingdom in Korean history that Koreans are very proud of. It managed to unite the peninsula for the first time, and is therefore considered very important. It's also the name of a large hotel in downtown Seoul:

신라 [실래]

Understanding the Korean World

Business cards are essential to doing business in Korea. Not carrying them is like heading to a war without bullets. Relationships are the key to business here (even more so than in other countries) and cards are the beginning of a relationship. If you want to meet the people who can help you accomplish your goals you need to have them remember you and a business card is the best way. Handing them out is, of course, an art.

When you receive or hand out a business card you should use two hands to receive it from or hand it to someone, in the same way that you should shake hands using two hands when you meet someone. It is also a little rude not to hand your own card back when you have received a card from someone else. If you don't have one or don't want to give one out to someone you don't know well, search through your pockets as if you are looking for one, and then make some excuse like, "They're in my other jacket." Or just use John's straightforward excuse: "지금 명함이 없기 때문에 못 드려요."

Exercises

 Answer using the words, and the time period + 동안.

1. 어제, 세 시간, 공부하다

2. 다음 달, 1주일, 서울, 있다

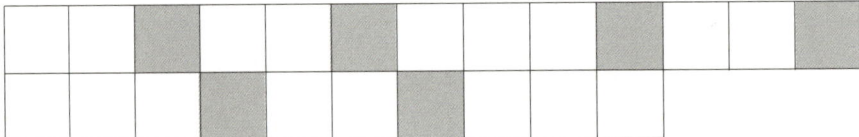

3. 내년, 6개월, 여행하다

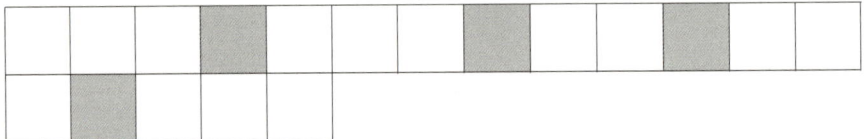

4. 그동안, 좋다

나 Use the given word plus N 때문에 to explain why.

1. 왜 못 가요? (학교)

_____

2. 그 책을 왜 샀어요? (싸다)

_____

3. 그 학교 왜 다녔어요? (친구)

_____

4. 왜 그 일을 해요? (돈)

_____

다 Practice the following situation with a friend.

It's time to say good-bye to your Korean teacher. Say your good-byes and assure her/him that you will be keeping in touch.

Study Tip

It's All About the Input

As the book comes to a close and I prepare to send you off into the real Korean-language world, I have one last major piece of advice: focus on input. When I say input, I'm talking about the receptive/passive skills: listening and reading. The input also needs to be at a level that is accessible to you. Sitting around watching the TV for 10 hours will not be as beneficial as listening to a beginner's cassette tapes for 5 hours. Reading a Korean novel probably won't help you yet, but reading an advertisement on the subway usually will.

Find accessible sources anywhere you can, and make them interesting. Most adults will find a catalog more interesting to read than a book of fairy tales. Many techies will find a tour around 용산전자상가 (Yong-san Electronics Market) more fruitful than a trip to the zoo. I have a friend who loves Korean comic books and his reading is great. Those comic books bore me to death, but I try to read the newspaper whenever I can. Stick with things of significance to you and you will learn more and remember them better.

And the best input is spending time with Koreans who are interested in helping you become a better Korean speaker. And not just studying in language lessons but also in social circumstances. I used to spend hours sitting around with Korean friends listening to their conversation, writing down words, guessing at meaning, but hardly saying a word. There are always good people out there who enjoy helping others. And many Koreans are still very grateful to have a foreigner studying their language. Trust me: the benefits you receive will provide you with a phenomenal return on your investment.

Answer Key

Chapter 1

가 1. 안녕하세요?
2. 안녕히 계세요.
3. 안녕히 가세요.
4. 한국말을 잘 몰라요.
5. 안녕히 가세요.

나 1. 몰라요.
2. 괜찮아요.
3. 고맙습니다.
4. 한국말을 잘 몰라요.
5. 안녕하세요?

Chapter 2

가 1. 이거 얼마예요?
2. 그거 얼마예요?
3. 저거 얼마예요?

나 1. 영어를 배우세요.
2. 가세요.
3. 주세요.
4. 한국말을 공부하세요.
5. 받으세요.

다 1. 칠백이십오
2. 구십팔
3. 육천오백삼십팔
4. 칠만 구천사백삼십오
5. 오십사만 구천이백삼십칠

Chapter 3

가 1. 이
2. 가
3. 이
4. 가
5. 가

나 1. 호주가 어디에 있어요?
2. 한국사람이 없어요.
3. 식당이 어디에 있어요?
4. 화장실이 어디에 있어요?

다 1. 세 시 삼십 분
2. 여덟 시 이십칠 분
3. 아홉 시 삼십일 분
4. 열한 시 오십 분
5. 열 시 십 분

Chapter 4

가 1. 에
2. 에서
3. 에서
4. 에서
5. 에

나 1. 존이 한국말을 공부해요.
2. 유식이 남대문에서 일해요.
3. 존이 유식을 만나요.

다 1. ~에서 공부해요.
2. ~에서 만나요.
3. ~에서 일해요.

Chapter 5

가 1. 가, 를
2. 가, 을

3. 이, 을
4. 이, 를

나 1. 만나요.
2. 읽어요.
3. 좋아요.
4. 줘요.
5. 와요.

다 1. 김치를 (안) 좋아해요.
2. 운동을 (안) 좋아해요.
3. 한국 노래를 (안) 좋아해요.

Chapter 6

가 1. 그 사람을 만나고 싶어요.
2. 편의점에 가고 싶어요.
3. 한국말을 공부하고 싶어요.

나 1. 그 영화가 좋으니까 보세요.
2. 비싸니까 좀 깎아 주세요.
3. 배고프니까 레스토랑에 가요.
4. 지금 바쁘니까 이따가 만나요.

다 1. 나빠요.
2. 아파요.
3. 써요.
4. 배가 고파요.

Chapter 7

가 1. 오시겠어요?
2. 가시겠어요?
3. 드시겠어요?
4. 주시겠어요?

나 1. 숙제를 하고 오세요.
2. 고추장을 빼고 주세요.
3. 밥을 먹고 만나요.

다 1. 먹을까요?
2. 쉴까요?
3. 갈까요?

Chapter 8

가 1. 어렵죠?
2. 맛있죠?
3. 맵죠?
4. 모르죠?

나 1. 어려워요.
2. 쉬워요.
3. 몰라요.
4. 빨라요.

다 1. 배부르지 않아요.
2. 뜨겁지 않아요.
3. 덥지 않아요.
4. 힘들지 않아요.

Chapter 9

가 1. 왼쪽으로 가 주세요.
2. 오른쪽으로 가 주세요.
3. 직진해 주세요.

나 1. 어디 가세요?
2. 뭘 공부하세요?
3. 추우세요?
4. 운동을 정말 잘 하세요.

다
1. 맛이 있네요.
2. 어렵네요.
3. 배부르네요.
4. 빠르네요.

라
1. 목욕탕에 못 가요.
2. 숙제를 못해요.
3. 친구를 못 만나요.

Chapter 10

가
1. 했어요.
2. 봤어요.
3. 왔어요.
4. 읽었어요.

나
1. 밥 먹으러 식당에 가요.
2. 우유를 사러 슈퍼에 가요.
3. 공부하러 도서관에 가요.

다
1. 오늘 밤에 전화할게요.
2. 내일 일찍 올게요.
3. 한국말을 열심히 공부할게요.
4. 조금 이따가 갈게요.

Chapter 11

가
1. 맛이 있는데요.
2. 공부했는데요.
3. 만났는데요.

나
1. 금요일이나 토요일에 가요?
2. 불고기나 갈비를 먹을까요?
3. 여섯 시나 일곱 시에 만날까요?

다
1. 커피숍에서 이야기합시다.

2. 쉽시다.
3. 닭갈비를 먹읍시다.
4. 지하철을 탑시다.
5. 집에서 책을 읽읍시다.

Chapter 12

가
1. 냉면을 먹을 수 있어요.
2. 한국말을 할 수 있어요.
3. 화요일에 만날 수 있어요.

나
1. 술을 마실 수 없어요.
2. 지금 나갈 수 없어요.
3. 중국어를 할 수 없어요.

다
1. 한국말을 잘 하면 한국 생활이 더 재미있어요.
2. 기차를 타면 더 빨라요.
3. 숙제를 하면 많이 배워요.

라
1. 숙제를 해야 돼요.
2. 5호선을 타야 돼요.
3. 한글을 배워야 돼요.

Chapter 13

가
1. 종이 세 장 주시겠어요?
2. 맥주 네 병 주시겠어요?
3. 와인 두 잔 주시겠어요?

나
1. 하얀색으로 할게요.
2. 작은 것으로 주세요.
3. 앞자리로 할게요.

다
1. 하얀색은 있는데 검은색이 없어요.
2. 어려운데 할 수 있어요.

3. 숙제를 했는데 이해할 수 없어요.
4. 와인인데 술이 없어요.

Chapter 14

가 1. 샤워할 거예요.
2. 더울 거예요.
3. 춤을 출 거예요.

나 1. 내려요.
2. 다녀요.
3. 기다려요.
4. 마셔요.

다 1. 공부하기가 어려워요/재미있어요/쉬워요.
2. 일하기가 힘들어요/안 힘들어요/재미있어요.
3. 서울에서 운전하기가 어려워요/힘들어요/무서워요.

Chapter 15

가 1. 존이 술을 (안) 마신 것 같아요.
2. 진호가 숙제를 (안) 한 것 같아요.
3. 그 학생이 책을 (안) 읽은 것 같아요.

나 1. 텔레비전 보는 것 같아요.
2. 버스를 타는 것 같아요.
3. 지금 뭐 먹는 것 같아요.

다 1. 존이 늦을 것 같아요.
2. 그 남자가 운동을 잘 할 것 같아요.
3. 비가 올 것 같아요.

Chapter 16

가 1. 여름에 존이 여행하려고 해요.
2. 오늘 6시에 친구를 만나려고 해요.
3. 혜숙 씨가 이따가 공부하려고 해요.
4. 선생님이 책을 읽으려고 해요.

나 1. 부터, 까지
2. 에서, 까지
3. 에서, 까지
4. 부터, 까지

Chapter 17

가 1. 회사라고 해요.
2. 집이라고 해요.
3. 도서관이라고 해요.

나 1. 성함이 어떻게 되세요?
2. 가족이 어떻게 되세요?
3. 나이가 어떻게 되세요?
   (연세가 어떻게 되세요?)

Chapter 18

가 1. 돈은 많이 버는데 시간이 없어요.
2. 어디 사세요?
3. 신촌에서 사니까 매일 놀아요.
4. 매일 노니까 돈을 못 벌어요.

나 1. 돈이 있었으면 좋겠어요.
2. 예뻤으면 좋겠어요.
3. 한국말을 잘 할 수 있었으면 좋겠어요.
4. 노래를 잘 했으면 좋겠어요.

Chapter 19

가 1. 같이 밥 먹을래요?
2. 농구할래요?
3. 이 셔츠 입을래요?

나 1. 학교에 갈래요.
2. 학교에서 축구할래요.
3. 바닷가에서 수영할래요.

다 1. 이 찌개 먹어도 돼요?
2. 그 치마 입어도 돼요?
3. 내일 학교에 안 나와도 돼요?
4. 와인 좀 마셔도 돼요?

Chapter 20

가 1. 어제 세 시간 동안 공부했어요.
2. 다음 달에 1주일 동안 서울에 있을 거예요.
3. 내년에 6개월 동안 여행할 거예요.
4. 그동안 좋았어요.

나 1. 학교 때문에 못 가요.
2. 싸기 때문에 샀어요.
3. 친구 때문에 다녔어요.
4. 돈 때문에 그 일을 해요.

Index

ㄱ

가게 ... 22, 65
가격 ... 55
가구 ... 213
가까운 ... 161
가깝다 ... 161
가끔 ... 86, 87
가다 ... 21, 46, 47
가도 돼요? ... 232
가려고 해요. ... 202
가수 ... 77
가슴 ... 99
가을 ... 181
가족 ... 222
간호사 ... 77
갈비 ... 109
갈색 ... 55
갈아타다 ... 160
감기 ... 190
감기에 걸렸어요 ... 190
감기에 걸리다 ... 191
감동적이다 ... 171
감사합니다 ... 46
감자 ... 109
값 ... 55
(값이) 나오다 ... 139
강 ... 29
강사 ... 77
같이 ... 86
개 ... 171
거 ... 54
건물 ... 65
것 ... 54

거기 ... 21
거실 ... 203
거의 ... 203
걷다 ... 129
걸리다 ... 202
검은색 ... 55
게임 ... 86
겨울 ... 181
경찰 ... 77
계단 ... 161
계속 가다 ... 139
계시다 ... 46
계절 ... 181
V고 ... 108
V고 싶다 ... 98
V고 있다 ... 150
고급 ... 77
고기 ... 108
고등학교 ... 77
고모 ... 223
고추 ... 28, 109
곳 ... 180
공부하다 ... 55, 76
공연 ... 151
공포 영화 ... 171
과식하다 ... 99
과일 ... 109
관광 ... 151
괜찮아요 ... 35, 46
교수 ... 77
교통 ... 129
구 ... 25, 31
구경하고 싶어요 ... 98
구경하다 ... 98, 203

구두	25, 233
9월	181
굵다	99
귀	99
귀걸이	243
귀엽다	233
귤	109
그 N	55
그 사람	55
그것	55
그곳	55
그냥	150
그동안	242
그동안 재미있었어요	242
그때	242
그때 주세요	242
그래서	25
그래요?	170
그런데	64
그렇게	150
그렇게 맵지 않아요	118
그렇게 합시다	150
그렇게 해야 될 것 같아요	190
극장	86
금방	99, 180
금요일	87
V기 싫어요	180
기다리다	22, 108, 180
기사	128
기차	129
기차표	28
김치찌개	109
N까지	202
깎다	54, 55
깎아 주세요	54
깨끗하다	35
꼭	242
꼭 전화할게요	242
꿰다	35

ㄴ

나라	21
나쁘다	35
나오다	138
나이	212
나이가 어떻게 되세요?	212
나중에	99
날씨	180
남동생	223
남자	64, 65
내과 의사	191
내년	151
내다	22
내리다	22, 138, 139
내릴게요	138
내일	151
너무	54, 118, 223
너무 매워요	118
너무 비싸요	54
너무 추워요	180
네	21, 46
V네요	128
넷	31
년생	212
~년생이에요	212
노란색	55
노래	87

녹색	55
녹차	65
놀다	223, 242
놀러 오세요	242
누구	25, 150
누구세요?	150
누나	222, 223
눈	99, 180
눈이 올 거예요	180
느낌	119

ㄷ

다	21, 138
다니다	21
다리	21, 99
다섯	31
다시	25
다음	128
다음 달	151
다음 주	151
다음에 봐요!	242
달다	119
닭	109
닭갈비	109
닭고기	109
당근	109
대학교	76, 77
더 A/V	160
더운	181
덥다	119, 181
N도	76
도서관	65
도움	190
도움이 안 돼요	190
도착	161
도착하다	161
독일	47
독일사람	47
독일어	47
돌아오다	202
돕다	202
동	29
동생	222
돼지	109
돼지고기	109
되다	160, 190, 212
된장	108
된장찌개	109
두 시간 반 걸려요	202
둘	31
뒤(쪽)	129
뒤에	129
드라마	171
드리다	108
드시다	108
들	86
디비디	139
따뜻하다	180, 181
따뜻한	181
딸	223
딸기	109
또	242
뛰다	129
뜨겁다	35, 119

ㄹ

라디오 · 139
러시아 · 47
러시아사람 · 47
러시아어 · 47
레스토랑 · 65

ㅁ

마다 · 21
마시다 · 25
마음 · 232
마음에 들어요 · 232
마흔 · 213
막내 · 222, 223
만 · 54, 212
만나다 · 76, 86
만나서 반갑습니다 · 76
만으로 ~살이에요 · 212
만화책 · 87
맛 · 118, 119
맛없다 · 119
맛이 없다 · 119
맛이 있다 · 119
맛(이) 있어요 · 118
맛있다 · 119
매 · 86
매년 · 87
매달 · 87
매번 · 87
매우 · 223
매월 · 87
매일 · 87
매주 · 87
매진되다 · 170
매표소 · 161
맥주 · 65
맵다 · 118, 119
머리 · 22, 99, 190
머리가 아파요 · 190
먹고 싶어요 · 98
먼 · 161
멀다 · 160, 161
멋있다 · 233
메뉴 · 108
며칠 · 202
며칠에 가려고 해요? · 202
명 · 171
명함 · 242
몇 · 64
몇 살이에요? · 213
몇 시예요? · 64
모르다 · 26, 46
모자 · 26, 233
모텔 · 203
목 · 99
목걸이 · 243
목도리 · 243
목요일 · 87
몰라요 · 46
몸 · 99
못생겼다 · 233
못했어요 · 170
무엇을 · 98
문구 · 171
문자 · 242
문자로 보낼게요 · 242

물 65, 109
물고기 109
뭐 하고 싶어요? 98
뭐 하고 있어요? 150
뭐 해요? 150
뭘 98
뭘 드릴까요? 108
뮤지컬 151
미국 47
미국사람 47
미니스커트 233

ㅂ

바가지 55
바가지 쓰다 55
바꾸다 150, 151
바지 233
밖에 129
반갑다 76
반바지 233
반지 243
받다 55
밥 108
방 29
배 98, 109, 129
배가 고파요 98
배가 고프다 99
배가 부르다 99
배가 아프다 191
배고프다 99
배부르다 99, 118
배불러요? 118
배불러요 118

배우 77
배우다 55
백 213
백화점 65
버스 129, 160
번호 242
벌다 223
벗다 233
베트남 47
베트남사람 47
베트남어 47
별로 안 86
별로 안 좋아해요 86
별말씀을요 232
병 171
병원 190, 191
보내다 25, 242
보다 25, 86
보통 86, 87
복잡하다 98
봄 180, 181
봐요 35
부모(님) 222
부엌 203
분 171
불고기 109
붓다 191
비디오 26, 139
비비다 108
비빔밥 109
비서 77
비싸다 54, 55
비자 25
비평 171

비행기	129
빌딩	64
빨간색	55
빨리	35, 138, 139
N 빼고 주세요	108
빼다	108

ㅅ

사	30
사과	109
사다	26
4월	181
사이에	129
산부인과 의사	191
산책하다	129, 232
산책할래요?	232
살	212, 213
살다	222, 223
삼	30
3월	181
삼촌	223
상관	232
상관없어요	232
상추	109
생각	86
생선	109
서랍장	213
서른	213
선글라스	232, 233
선로	161
선생님	31, 77
성별	65
성함	212

성함이 어떻게 되세요?	212
세	213
세우다	138, 139
세워 주세요	138
셋	31
소	109
소고기	109
소아과 의사	191
소주	65
소파	213
속이 쓰리다	191
손님	139
쇼핑	150, 151
숍	64
수요일	87
숙박	203
술	65
슈퍼(마켓)	65
쉰	213
쉽다	119
스물	213
스웨터	233
스페인	47
스페인사람	47
스페인어	47
습니다	76
승객	139
시	64
시간	202
V시겠어요?	108
시계	243
시다	119
시원하다	181
시원한	181

10월	181
시장	65
식당	65
식사	119, 150
식탁	213
신다	233
신문	87, 150
실례	64
실례지만	64
심심하다	150
심심해요	150
십	31
12월	181
11월	181
싱겁다	119
싸다	55
쌀쌀하다	181
쌀쌀한	181
쑤시다	191
쓰다	119, 233
씨	76

ㅇ

아까	99
아니오	46
아들	223
아래	25
아래에	129
아름답다	233
아마	242
아마 갈 거예요	242
아버지	223
아빠	223
아이	26
아저씨	138
아주	25, 118, 222, 223, 232
아줌마	54
아침	31, 119
아프다	190
아홉	31
아흔	213
안	86
안경	243
안녕	31, 46
안녕하세요	46
안녕히 가세요	46
안녕히 계세요	46
안방	203
안에	129
안전선	161
알다	160
알았어요	160
앞(쪽)	129
앞에	128, 129
액세서리	243
액션 영화	171
야채	109
약	190
약국	191
약을 먹어요	190
양주	65
양파	109
애기	29
어디	25, 64
어디 사세요?	222
어디 아파요?	191
어디에 있어요?	64

어떤	76, 138	여기에 있어요	64
어떤 일을 해요?	76	여기에서 멀어요?	160
어떻게	160	여기요!	54
어떻게 오셨어요?	202	여덟	31
어떻다	180	여동생	223
어렵다	119	여든	213
어머니	223	여름	181
어서	202	여보세요?	150
어서 오세요	202	여섯	31
어울리다	232	V여/아/어 주다	128
어제	151	V여/아/어도 돼요?	232
언니	222, 223	V여/아/어서	76
언제	151	여자	29, 65
얼마	54	여행	31, 203
얼마나	202	여행하다	203
얼마나 걸려요?	161	역	160
얼마예요?	54	연극	151
엄마	223	연락처	242
없다	64	연락하다	242
없어요	64	연필	171
엉덩이	99	열	31, 213
N에 가고 싶어요	98	였/았/었어요	138
P에 어떻게 가요?	160	V였/았/었으면 좋겠어요	222
N에 살아요	222	영	29
P에서	202	영국	47
P_1에서 P_2까지 얼마나 걸려요?	202	영국사람	47
N에(서) 사세요?	222	영어	47
N에서 왔어요	138	영화	86, 87
SF(에스에프) 영화	171	영화가 어땠어요?	170
에스컬레이터	161	영화를 봐요	86
엘리베이터	161	옆	64
여관	203	옆에	129
여기	54	예매하다	170
여기 있어요	108, 138	예매했어요?	170

예쁘다	232, 233	왼	128
예순	213	왼(쪽)	129
예약	202, 203	왼쪽으로 가 주세요	128
예약을 취소하다	203	우리	138
예약하다	203	우유	29, 65
예전에	99	운동	87
오	30	운동화	233
오늘	150, 151, 170	운전하다	129
오다	47	원	35, 54
오렌지	109	~원 나왔어요	138
오른	128	월	180
오른(쪽)	129	월요일	87
오른쪽으로 가 주세요	128	위에	129
오빠	212, 222, 223	위험	35
오이	26	6월	181
5월	181	유치원	77
오페라	151	육	30
오후	232	(으)ㄴ	170
온도	181	V(으)니까	98
온돌방	203	(으)ㄹ 거예요	180
올해	151	V(으)ㄹ 수 있다	160
옷	233	V(으)ㄹ까요?	108
옷장	203	V(으)ㄹ래요?	232
와	128	V(으)려고 하다	202
와이셔츠	233	N(으)로	25, 128
와인	65	T(으)로 어떻게 가요?	160
왕복	203	V(으)ㅂ시다	150
왜?	35	V(으)세요?	128
외과 의사	191	은/는	128
외국인	35	은/는데요	150
외동딸	223	V은/는/을 것 같다	190
외동아들	223	은행	65
외모	233	은행원	77
외삼촌	223	N(을/를) 사야 돼요.	170

N을/를 주시겠어요?	108
음료	65
음악회	151
의사	35, 77, 191
의자	213
이	25, 30, 54, 55
이 사람	55
N이/가 금방 올 거예요	180
N이/가 싫어요	180
N이/가 없으니까 지금 드릴 수 없어요	242
N이/가 있었으면 좋겠어요	222
이것	55
이곳	55
N(이)나 N	150
이다	25, 54
~(이)라고 하다	212
이따	160
이따 봐요	160
이따가	98, 99
이따가 가요	98
이름	76
이모	223
이번 달	151
이번 주	151
이비인후과 의사	191
이상하네요	190
이상하다	190
2월	181
이제	98
인사동	98
일	30, 76, 138, 202
일곱	31
일본	47
일본사람	47
일본어	47
1월	181
일요일	86, 87
일흔	213
읽다	86
입	99
입다	233
있다	64

ㅈ

자다	26
자매	223
자주	87
작년	151
잔	171
잘	46, 128
잘 어울려요	232
잘생겼다	232, 233
잘생겼어요	232
잠깐	151
잠깐 멈추다	139
잠시	108
잠시만 기다리세요	108
잡지	87
장	170, 171
장갑	243
장남	223
장녀	223
재미없다	171
재미있다	171
재미있었어요	170
재킷	233
저	55, 76

저 사람	55	좋아요	54
저것	55	좋아하다	86
저곳	55	좋은 생각이에요	86
저기	64	죄송하다	170
저기에 있어요	64	죄송합니다	170
저기요!	54	주	86, 170
저녁	31, 119	주다	54
저는 N을/를 좋아해요	86	주말에 뭐 해요?	86
저는 ~(이)라고 해요	212	주문하다	108
저도요	76	주문하시겠어요?	108
전데요	150	주사	191
전시회	151	주세요	54
전화	242	주스	65
(전화) 잘못 걸다	151	중국	47
전화번호 가르쳐 주면 연락할게요	242	중국사람	47
전화번호 가르쳐 주세요	242	중국어	47
점심	31, 119	중급	77
정거장	160	중학교	77
~ 정거장만 가면 돼요	160	증상	191
정도	202, 203	지금	64
정말	86, 223	지난	170
정말 잘 해요	128	지난 달	151
제	76	지난 주	151
제 이름은 ~이에요/예요	76	지루하다	171
제가 N을/를 좋아해요	86	N/V지만	64
조금	98, 118, 180, 223	지우개	171
조금 전에	99	지하철	129, 160, 161
조금만 기다려요	180	지하철을 타면 더 빨라요	160
조깅하다	129	직업	77
좀	54, 98, 108, 150	직진하다	128
P 좀 바꿔 주시겠어요?	150	직진해 주세요	128
종업원	108	진짜	223, 232
종이	171	진찰	191
좋다	54	집	138, 203

짜다 118, 119
쪽 128
쯤 203
찌개 108

ㅊ

차 65
차갑다 119
차다 233
차례 28
책 86, 87
책상 213
책을 읽어요 86
책장 213
천천히 139
청바지 233
쳐다보다 28
초급 77
초등학교 77
추운 181
출발 161
출발하다 161, 202
춤 87
춤다 119, 180, 181
취미 86, 87
치료 191
치마 232, 233
친구 86
칠 30
7월 181
침대 203
침실 203

ㅋ

카세트 139
캐나다 47, 138
캐나다사람 47
커피 64, 65
커피숍 65
컴퓨터 86
컴퓨터 게임 87
켜다 28
코 99
코너 128
코믹 영화 171
코트 28
콘서트 151
콜라 65
콧물 190
콧물이 나와요 190
콩 29

ㅌ

타다 129, 139
탁자 213
택시 128, 129
(택시) 기사 139
택시 요금 139
택시비 139
테이블 213
텔레비전 139
토요일 86, 87
통화중이다 151
튜브 28
티셔츠 233

ㅍ

파	109
파란색	55
팔	30, 99
8월	181
팔찌	243
펜	171
편도	203
편의점	65
폐	28
포도	28, 109
프랑스	47
프랑스사람	47
프랑스어	47
피곤하다	46

ㅎ

P하고 같이 살아요	222
하나	31
학교	77
학생	76, 138
학원	77
(한) 번	242
한국	31, 47
한국 나이	212
한국 나이로 ~살이에요	212
한국말	46, 128
한국말 잘 못해요	128
한국말을 잘 몰라요	46
한국사람	47
한국어	47
한식	109
N한테	232
할래요?	232
할머니	223
할아버지	223
항상	87
해도 돼요?	232
해요	76
혀	28
형	222, 223
형제	222, 223
형편없다	171
호선	160, 161
~호선으로 갈아타세요	160
호주	47
호주사람	47
호텔	203
혼자	222
홍차	65
화요일	87
화장실	64
회사	35
회사원	76, 77
효과	28
후	108
휴가	28
휴게소	29
흰색	55
힘들다	119